# MARRINER'S YARNS

# Marriner's Yarns

*The Story of the Keighley Knitting Wool Spinners*

George Ingle

PUBLICATION SUPPORTED BY A CONTRIBUTION FROM
THE PASOLD RESEARCH FUND

*Marriner's Yarns: The Story of the Keighley Knitting Wool Spinners*

First published in 2004 by
Carnegie Publishing Ltd,
Carnegie House, Chatsworth Road
Lancaster LA1 4SL
www.carnegiepublishing.com

© George Ingle 2004

Typeset and originated by
Carnegie Publishing

*Cataloguing-in-Publication data*
A catalogue record for this book is available from the British Library

ISBN 1-85936-103-X

Printed and bound in the UK by
Biddles Ltd, King's Lynn

# Contents

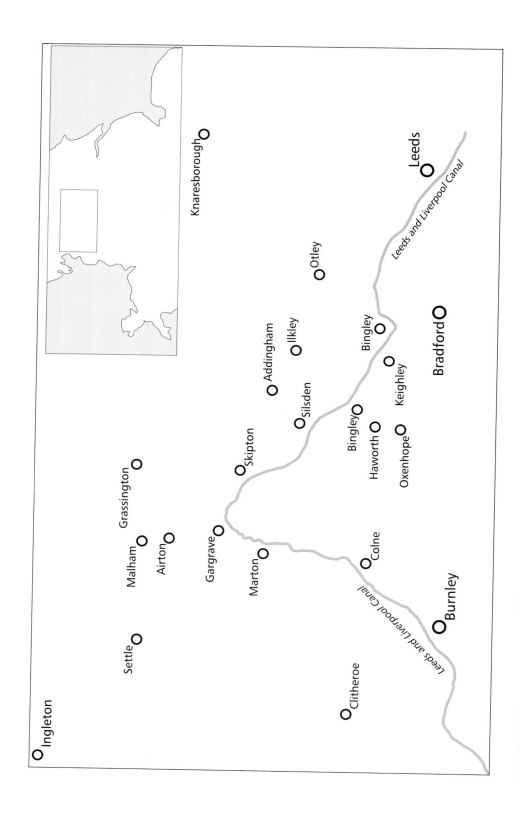

# Preface and acknowledgements

I N 1948, after the Second World War, the Economics Department of the University of Leeds began a survey of the wool textile industry. Many firms had given their records to be pulped as part of the war effort and this survey aimed to record, and, if possible, preserve those still held by the industry's old established firms. R V Marriner Ltd, of Greengate Mill, Keighley, did not respond in 1948 but, remembering the request, donated their ledgers and papers in 1963. The collection, now held by the Brotherton Library of the University of Leeds, comprises books, letters, diaries, plans, documents and papers relating to the activities of the Marriner family of Keighley as well as the Andertons of Bingley, the Listers of Frizinghall and the Spencers of Keighley. These families were all related by marriage. Only a part of the collection relates to the firm that became R V Marriner Ltd. The papers provided the basis for a thesis presented for the degree of MPhil at Leeds in 1974 under the supervision of Dr Gerard Turnbull, and this book has grown from it after an interval of many years.

This thesis covered a period of about a hundred years from 1784 to 1888 when two of the Marriner brothers quarrelled and split the business. Originally the firm was started for the purpose of spinning cotton, not worsted and for over thirty years Greengate Mill was one of hundreds of cotton spinning mills operating in Yorkshire. The scale of the industry at that time has been covered in *Yorkshire Cotton* published in 1997. Keighley was one of the main centres for the early cotton industry with thirty-four mills built by 1810. Those early years, together with the growth of the local worsted industry, the textile machinery industry and the associated machine tool industry are all recorded in John Hodgson's book *Textile Manufacture and other Industries in Keighley*, first published in 1879. A facsimile reprint was published in 1999 and many references are made to it in this work. A limited attempt has been made to to set the firm within its local community and within some of the movements which resulted from changes in technology early in the nineteenth century. The role of members of the Marriner family during those years has been given wherever possible. Good relations with their workpeople at the time continued through into the next century and still exist in the memories of those who worked at Greengate Mill.

This book covers a period of more than two hundred years, during which, five generations of the Marriner family controlled the business. They inherited one of the country's first cotton spinning firms which they changed over to worsted spinning, and upon which, during the nineteenth century, they built one of the town's most important businesses. Marriners soon produced a wide range of worsted yarns for both home and foreign markets, though changing circumstances eventually reduced output to hand-knitting wool. Following the Second World War Marriners entered the retail market and their own name was used in selling hand-knitting yarns. In many cupboards and drawers across the country old knitting patterns bearing their name can still be found. The Marriner family sold the firm in 1957 when demand was strong and production continued, but knitting as an activity has declined drastically over the years since, in line with the decline in the British textile industry. Further changes came in the 1980s but the strength of the Marriner name was such that a leading wholesaler in Wales took over the brand and still sells hand-knitting wool with a Marriner label. The original Greengate Mill, built for cotton spinning in 1784, was demolished following a disastrous fire in 1975.

I would like to acknowledge the willing co-operation of staff at the Brotherton Library for help, both recently, and in years gone by. Pauline Barfoot at Keighley Reference Library and Dale Keeton at Cliffe Castle Museum in Keighley have provided both help and encouragement. Ann Dinsdale, the librarian for the Bronte Society, provided detailed information about the Bronte link while Susan Marsden and members of the Keighley & District Family History Society provided assistance with the Marriner genealogy. Henry Hallam, a Marriner cousin, has added to the encouragement of the late John Marriner to enlarge on the original thesis. Dr Gill Cookson's original work on Keighley machine makers has been drawn on and her co-operation is appreciated. Duncan Lodge provided details of the Pollit & Wigzell mill engine and John Allison provided access to the Bradford Textile Archive. Robin Greenwood kindly gave me a copy of his monumental work on the Greenwood family. Bob Hartley, who worked for J W Allen Ltd., was able to provide information about the links beween Marriners and other companies in the 1970s and 1980s. Colin Shaw supplied examples of knitting leaflets and labels that his company now use with the Marrriner name. Much encouragement and assistance has come from Chris Aspin. His suggestions regarding the manuscript and knowledge of the early cotton industry have been invaluable in improving the accuracy and readability of the text. I am also grateful to the many people who worked at Greengate Mill for their memories and stories. Particular thanks go to Annie Lund for permission to use her poem, 'Mills' and article, 'The Old Mill on Fire'. Further information about hand knitting can be obtained from The Knitting & Crochet Guild while old knitting patterns are available from yesterknits. com. The errors and omissions are mine.

The late Eric Sigsworth started my original interest in textile history many years ago. His history of John Foster & Son Ltd, *Black Dyke Mills*, published in 1958, was an inspiration which I could never emulate. However, as my working life started at Keighley College, I have been pleased to be able to write this history of a well-known Keighley firm. Keighley was never one of the largest textile towns but it was often in the lead with technical innovation and education. The Marriner family played an important part in the development of the textile industry and of the town, which was proved by the two hundred years the firm existed. My work on the firm's records started forty years ago and it was always the wish of John Marriner, the last of the family to run the firm, that a book be published based on those records. After an interval of many years I have been able to accomplish this with the help of a grant from the Pasold Research Fund and I am most grateful for the Fund's help and support. John Marriner would have been pleased to see this record of the firm built up by his family.

The Marriner papers, which are held at the Brotherton Library at the University of Leeds, are well catalogued with a detailed index available. I have therefore not given the name or reference number for every document, ledger, letter or diary which has been drawn on for this account, as this would have been a rather tedious list. The catalogue was made some time after the original collection was given to the library. In its original condition the collection was delivered to the library covered in dust, in a variety of boxes, skeps and bundles, and as it had been rescued from a store-room at the mill. The current catalogue is therefore very useful. Where possible original documents and papers have been used for illustrations and I acknowledge with thanks those who have given permission to use copyright material

The illustrations are based on a variety of sources. I was able to take some photographs of Greengate Mill about 1963, just before John Marriner left the company. John Marriner also gave most of the original materials used for illustrations and over the years more have been collected. Every attempt has been made to trace ownership but if rights have been contravened apologies are offered. Full acknowledgement is made for the following: Marriner Papers, University of Leeds Library Business Archives, pp. 48, 60; Guildhall Library, London, p. 29; Kirklees Community History Service, p. 67; Bradford Art Galleries and Museums, pp. 80, 110, 153, 155; Keighley News, p. 135.

Inevitably the latter part of the book contains the most illustrations, but hopefully all add something to the story.

## Notes

### 1. Prices
Where possible, relevant prices or costs have been taken from the original documents and included in the text. These have been given in pounds, shillings and pence together with a metric equivalent. The problem with some of the smaller amounts is that the pound could, at the time, be divided into 960 farthings whereas now it is divided into 100 pence. During the eighteenth and nineteenth centuries prices for certain commodities and work done were charged to the nearest farthing, as price differentials were very keen. Some conversions are therefore approximate.

### 2. Timescale
The time-scale for this book stretches for over two hundred years so this

summary of the main changes in ownership and the people concerned may be of value.

| | |
|---|---|
| 1784 | Greengate Mill built by five partners for spinning cotton. |
| 1792 | Ann Flesher inherited a one-third share from her uncle, Abraham Smith, one of the original partners. |
| 1792 | Ann Flesher married William Marriner. |
| 1805 | William Marriner bought an additional one-sixth share. He died in 1809. |
| 1817 | Benjamin and William Marriner (sons of William and Ann) bought remaining shares and changed mill over to worsted spinning. |
| 1857 | William Marriner, who was unmarried, left the firm. |
| 1857 | Benjamin Marriner and his two sons, William Lister Marriner and his younger brother Edward (from 1862) ran the firm. Benjamin died in 1866. |
| 1888 | William Lister Marriner and Edward Marriner divided the firm and Edward Mariner founded a separate company. He died in 1912. |
| 1888 | Firm continued as Marriner, Son & Naylor. This was William Lister Marriner, his son Henry who continued as a partner until after 1908 and William Naylor, a former manager. |
| 1908 | Raymond Vincent Marriner, another son of Lister Marriner, was brought in to take over the running of the firm which then took his name. |
| 1934 | John Marriner, son of Raymond Vincent Marriner, joined the firm. |
| 1957 | Firm bought by Union International Ltd. Marriner ownership ended but trading name retained. John Marriner remained as manager from 1957 until 1963. |
| 1975 | Serious fire at Greengate Mill with many surviving buildings later demolished. Firm moved to Knowle Mill, Keighley. |
| 1983 | Assets and goodwill of R V Marriner Ltd sold to Marriner Yarns Ltd. |
| 1985 | Marriner Yarns Ltd in liquidation. Name bought by Shaws (Cardiff) Ltd who trade as Shaws the Drapers. Continued selling hand-knitting yarn with Marriner label. |
| 1995 | R V Marriner Ltd dissolved. (Had not traded since 1983) |
| 2003 | Hand-knitting yarn with the Marriner brand name continues to be sold by Shaws in South Wales but spun by Carter & Parker (Wendy Wools) Ltd. |

## 3. Trading Names

| | |
|---|---|
| 1784–1805 | Watson, Blakeys, Smith & Greenwood, then Blakeys, Smith & Watson, then Watson, Blakeys & Marriner |
| 1805–1817 | Blakeys & Marriner |
| 1817–1857 | B & W Marriner (Benjamin and William Marriner) |
| 1857–1888 | B & W Marriner (Benjamin and William Lister Marriner) |
| 1888–1908 | Marriner, Son & Naylor |
| 1908–1924 | R V Marriner |
| 1924–1995 | R V Marriner Ltd (stopped trading 1983) |
| 1983–1985 | Marriner Yarns Ltd |
| 1985– | to date Shaws (Cardiff) Ltd. Selling hand-knitting yarn with Marriner label |

## Mills

The shrill siren screams,
Piercing the darkness
Of the early morn
The clatter of clogs
Rattles the setts,
The lacy shawl, torn
And ragged, droops o'er
The tiny figure, hurrying,
Always hurrying,
To the rhythm of machines

Clogs echo on wood;
Machines take over
Susan's fingers, heart and soul.
Threads flying.
Knots tying
Waste fills – nostrils.
Mouth – tastes waste.
Bobbins clang.
Doffers bang;
The mills of yesteryear.

Modern miss in jeans
Minds the new machines
Shining, streamlined, clean.
Everywhere
Vacuumed air.
Teabreak – in between
Tying ends.
A chat with friends,
With meals in a canteen ...
The 'factories' of today.

Poem by Annie Lund who worked at Marriners from 1932 to 1939.
First published by Arnold-Wheaton in *Wheels. An Industrial Anthology.* 1982.

# Marriner's

## Heritage & Nylon

### 7-9, 10-12 & 13-15 years

6D

Marriner Knitting Wools

N° 192

CHAPTER ONE

# Keighley in 1780

THE TOWN OF Keighley in the West Riding of Yorkshire has as its motto the phrase 'By Worth'. Apart from the hope that the town will be judged by its merit, the choice of words emphasises the importance for the growth of Keighley of the River Worth on which it stands. The Worth was the source of power for Keighley's early textile mills, which were built in the late eighteenth and early nineteenth centuries. This river, with its tributary, the North Beck, flows into the river Aire and provided sites for a concentration of new textile mills that brought the industrial revolution to the area. For Keighley this revolution began in 1780 and was part of the national change to factory production from hand operated machines and tools. In the textile industry this was a long process which took nearly one hundred years to complete. Keighley was the first town in Yorkshire to be affected by the major changes in textile manufacture and was instrumental in driving the changes forward in the years that followed. These changes came slowly and were not taken up uniformly. Because machines displaced hand labour, there was opposition, which was frequently violent, and the changes always resulted in large-scale industrial adjustments, social change and population movement. The sequence of changes, which lies behind the first sections of this book, started firstly in the spinning process, which then produced pressure to mechanise weaving which in turn, for the worsted industry, led to the mechanisation of combing. Alongside these major changes came changes in dyeing and printing. Because of the different natures of the natural textile fibres such as cotton, wool, flax and silk, related mechanisation proceeded at different rates and this, too, is illustrated by the adaptation of new methods of production in the Keighley area.

The population of the parish of Keighley in 1750 was 2,845. Twenty years later is was 3,650 and in 1780 when the first mill was built it was 4,000. The first census in 1801 gave a figure of 5,745 so the population doubled in the second half of the eighteenth century. One factor which stimulated the development of Keighley was the opening of the section of the Leeds and Liverpool Canal between Skipton and Bingley in 1773. Easier access to other parts of Yorkshire was extended in 1774 when a connection was made with the Bradford Canal and further reinforced in 1777 when the Leeds and Liverpool Canal was opened to Leeds, which was also the terminus of the Aire and Calder Navigation. However, although modern Keighley stretches across the Leeds and Liverpool Canal it did not do so in the 1770s. As a

Keighley's first railway station in 1847.

result there was a certain expense in carting goods from the canal warehouse at Stockbridge. Despite this, most heavy goods such as coal, wool, timber and iron were conveyed by canal. This connection with Bradford, Leeds, East Yorkshire and later, when the canal was completed over the Pennines, with Lancashire, was of great benefit to Keighley before the coming of the railway in 1847 and greatly helped the town's industrial development.

## The worsted industry

In 1780 the main manufacturing industry in and around Keighley was worsted with most men in the town employed as hand-combers or hand loom weavers. Keighley lay at the western edge of the West Yorkshire worsted manufacturing area which stretched from Leeds and Wakefield in the east, to Otley in the north, and then across to Halifax. Several years previously the Yorkshire worsted industry had started to equal the output of East Anglia, and Keighley played an important part in this and future expansion.[1] The earlier manufacture of woollen cloth in Keighley remained only in names such as Walk Mill, Stockbridge and several 'Tenter Crofts'.[2] The organisation of the worsted industry in the locality was based on 'manufacturers' who were at the centre of a complex network of transactions. Their capital was required to finance the working of the wool through the three main processes of combing, spinning and weaving, which were all done by hand. After the wool was bought and sorted it had to be combed, which would have been done locally in Keighley or nearby. Some was often combed at the manufacturer's warehouse.

For the next process large numbers of hand-spinners were required which meant that the combed wool had to be distributed over a wide area before the resulting yarn could be brought back to the warehouse and taken away again by the hand loom weavers. These processes were quite separate in their requirements and often geographically distinct. The equipment used was relatively simple, cheap and easy to make, but it was difficult for workers to rise above the ranks of 'comber', 'spinster' or 'weaver', although in good times some weavers did manage to join the numbers of small manufacturers. Accounts of the time describe the links between seasonal small scale farming for many of the men, with their womenfolk and children taking care of the carding and spinning.

The manufacturers bought their wool from wool-staplers or direct from farms in East Yorkshire and Lincolnshire. Around 1800 there were a number of wool-staplers with warehouses in Keighley. Hodgson lists six or seven including David Spencer whose daughter married Benjamin Marriner in 1822. These staplers also bought their wool in East Yorkshire, Lincolnshire or Leicestershire, but by holding stocks were able to supply the smaller manufacturers and saved the larger manufacturers having to hold large quantities themselves. Wool-staplers also operated in Bradford, Halifax and Wakefield as well as smaller places such as Sutton and Cringles near Silsden.[3]

The Keighley manufacturers produced a variety of worsted pieces of different lengths and widths. Hodgson lists some of these:

**Shalloons**

Used for women's dresses. A great number were dyed scarlet and exported to Turkey.

**Says**

Heavier than shalloons and largely exported to Spain, Portugal and Italy to make priests' robes.

**Russels**

Used for ladies' petticoats, boots, shoes and men's waistcoats.

**Lastings**

A stout fabric only 18 inches wide.

**Drawboys**

These had a woven pattern which originally required the help of a boy with the weaving.

**Amens**

Were woven with a pattern.

**Callamancos**

Used for ladies' petticoats and chair seating

**Tammies**

Used for ladies' dresses with large numbers being exported.

Hand combers. Photograph of part of Lister Monument in Lister Park, Bradford.

**Wildbores**
Like a Tammie but made from lower quality wool

**Camlets**
In the home market they were used for making cloaks, but most were exported to China and the East Indies.

**Moreens**
Used for bed curtains and furniture.

**Bombazines**
These had a silk warp.[4]

The description of the use for each type of cloth, for example one cloth being used for both petticoats and chair seating, sounds strange to modern ears, but explains the huge demand for cotton cloth when that became cheap and widely available.

The principal market for the output of the Keighley manufacturers initially was Halifax, where the Piece Hall had been built in 1779 with over 300 rooms for local manufacturers to display their cloth. Many of the Keighley and Haworth manufacturers had rooms there and took their cloth weekly by cart or pack-horse. Merchants who dealt with the various finishing processes then bought the cloth and sold it on the home market or sent it abroad. Halifax Piece Hall gradually lost its position as the main outlet for Keighley worsted pieces after about 1800. To make up for some of the decline, cotton manufacturers were allowed to display their cloth there from 1805.[5] Bradford Piece Hall, which was built in 1773 and added to in 1780, then became the main market place for worsted cloth and Bradford went on to become the centre of the West Riding worsted industry.[6]

This three-stage organisation of the local worsted industry, and the hand processes, continued for many years after 1780. Indeed the structure of the industry late in the nineteenth century and into more modern times reflects this early separation of the three main processes although without the geographic spread. This separation was intensified by the introduction of mechanisation over several years and the length of time it took for the new machines to totally supersede hand production. One of the reasons was, that although there was a tremendous drive to innovate and introduce new machinery, the first examples were often clumsy and did not produce the quality that was required. Worsted spinning by power driven machine first started in Yorkshire at Addingham Low Mill in 1787 and it followed at Bridgehouse Mill in Haworth in 1788 but it was not until 1820 that the domestic spinning of worsted yarn was extinct.[7] Similarly the first attempts to use the power loom in the worsted industry occurred in 1822 but Keighley manufacturers only dared to introduce them in the 1830s with Marriners deciding not to use them at all. Despite the advantages of the power loom, hand loom weaving continued until the 1850s for a variety of reasons. The mechanisation of the combing process proved even harder to perfect. Early examples of the 'Big Ben' machine were available in the 1790s, but it was not until the 1850s that excellent results were obtained with the Noble comb. This time the demise of the job of the hand comber was almost immediate.

## Local manufacturers

All these changes can be seen later in the business activities of various members of the Marriner family, but records exist of the organisation of the local worsted industry at a slightly earlier period. William Greenwood of Oxenhope near Keighley died in 1779 and until then he had been both a farmer and producer of worsted and woollen yarn. He had a warehouse full of wool, tops, noils and yarn. There was a combing shop with 12 pairs of combs and combing stocks as well as soap, oil and dye to help clean, prepare and colour the yarn. Greenwood sold his yarn and was not involved in weaving. However, he had to supervise a wide variety of transactions from buying a range of raw materials to dealing with hand spinners over a wide area who were not under his immediate control. The only people under his immediate control were the wool combers and dyers. William Greenwood died before mechanisation came into the worsted industry, but his son John continued the business and built Old Oxenhope Mill in Hanging Gate Lane about 1800.

Another local man who was engaged in the worsted trade at the same time as William Greenwood was Robert Heaton of Ponden Hall. He also was a farmer, but did not stop at producing and selling worsted yarn for he organised the weaving of cloth. Details exist of his yarn being spun in Sawley, Rimington, Chatburn and Downham in the Pendle area of Lancashire as well as at Long Preston, Giggleswick and Rathmell in Ribblesdale. When the yarn was returned to Ponden it would be sorted into qualities, as the hand spinners could not produce a uniform product. Weaving was then probably done locally with the weavers coming to the warehouse to collect yarn and return cloth, which was then sent to Halifax for sale. Robert Heaton's worsted business expanded with increased sales until the late 1780s, but then, after a sudden decline, he and his son decided to enter the new industry which had started in Keighley – cotton spinning.[8]

Hodgson lists many worsted manufacturers who followed the pattern of business described above:

James Haggas ... while continuing the manufacturing business and cultivating the farm at Oakworth Hall, was also in the habit of going into Lincolnshire to buy his wool. The class of goods he made consisted of says, drawboys and shalloons, having his warehouse at Oakworth Hall where he stored his goods, sorted his wool and delivered out work to combers and weavers, selling his pieces at Halifax market.[9]

Mr John Clough ... was engaged in business as a manufacturer of stuff pieces, such as calimancos, plainbacks and wildbores, employing hand combers and hand loom weavers, and having his yarn spun by the hand spinning wheel one thread at a time. He was in the habit of taking his tops into the dales on horseback, and delivering them out in small quantities to hand spinners, or, like other manufacturers of the day, leaving a bag of tops with a village shopkeeper, and allowing a small commission for his trouble, and the shopkeepers were generally ready to undertake this business as it brought additional custom to the shop.[10]

Nathanial Walbank ... resided at Thwaites, where he employed both combers and weavers, and, like other manufacturers of that day, gave out his tops to hand spinners. The class of goods he principally made were drawboys ... He sold his goods on the Halifax market.[11]

## Cotton spinning

Across the Lancashire border the manufacture of cotton yarn and the weaving of cloth with a cotton weft and linen warp had arrived from East Anglia by 1600. The industry then developed and spread across the county with large numbers of people engaged in hand spinning, hand loom weaving and the various bleaching, dyeing and printing processes. Demand for this type of linen/cotton cloth continued to rise during the eighteenth century and eventually Hargreaves, Arkwright and Crompton developed spinning machines, which significantly increased both the quantity and quality of cotton yarn available. Cotton cloth could then be woven completely from the machine spun yarns without the need for linen warp, rendering it cheaper than the imported Indian cloth. However, until 1780 little or no cotton was processed in Yorkshire. It was the mechanisation of the spinning process, because of rising demand, and the rapid spread of the cotton industry to many parts of Britain that made Yorkshire, particularly the West Riding, a natural area for future development.

In 1768 Richard Arkwright moved from his home town of Preston to Nottingham where he settled not far from James Hargreaves who had also moved from Lancashire. Hargreaves found that his development of the jenny, which was a hand-powered spinning machine with eventually up to one hundred spindles, was not welcome in Lancashire. In 1768 a mob had attacked his home and destroyed a large number of machines he had under construction. Hargreaves had a partner in Nottingham, Thomas James, and they ran a small mill using his jenny. As a spinning machine it proved very useful for many years as it could spin fine yarn for weft and, although a hand

powered machine, was then widely used in West Yorkshire for spinning cotton and wool.

When Arkwright left Lancashire he had developed a spinning machine which he was able to develop with the financial backing of new partners in a safer environment. He went on to become a partner in ten mills in the Midlands, two in Scotland and two in Lancashire, Birkacre and Manchester. Arkwright had developed a series of machines that only needed relatively unskilled children to watch over all the processes for the production of yarn from raw cotton. He and his partners went on to make large amounts of money and thus generated a desire to emulate their achievements among others. To protect his position Arkwright had taken out his first patent in 1769 with others in 1778. However, opposition to Arkwright from his competitors grew and when it was proved that he had incorporated other inventors' ideas into his machines he was deprived of his patent rights.

Thomas Walshman, one of the partners at Arkwright's Birkacre mill, and two Preston spinners, George and William Clayton came to Keighley and took over the lease of the new Low Mill which had been built by Thomas Ramsden of Halifax. There is no record of why Ramsden was building this new mill in Keighley or why he was prepared to give up his lease although it may have been intended to be a wool scribbling mill. Claytons & Walshman entered into a licence agreement with Richard Arkwright and his Midland partners to operate this new cotton mill under Arkwright's patents, which related to carding, roving and spinning. Claytons & Walshman agreed to pay Richard Arkwright £4,200 plus £600 interest for the use of the patents which included help with the construction of the machinery and help with the training of the children and others who would operate the carding and spinning machines.

> Clayton & Walshman commenced cotton spinning on the 30 June, 1780, and the machinery for this mill was made under the direction of Sir Richard Arkwright; and, as it was the first cotton mill in the county, the proprietors sent a number of children and young persons to Arkwright's works at Cromford, in Derbyshire, to learn the various processes connected with cotton spinning, such as the minding and tending the carding, preparing and spinning machinery.[12]

Later, when Claytons & Walshman built another large mill at Langcliffe, near Settle, the children there came to Keighley Low Mill to learn the necessary skills.

The building of Low Mill started a boom in cotton spinning in Keighley. From 1780 the river Worth and North Beck in Keighley and Haworth provided the power for an increasing number of cotton mills. The cotton spinning business attracted both men and women in the area who had capital or land suitable for a mill. There was a rush to buy plots of land with water rights where the streams could be dammed and the water stored to provide a fall for a water wheel. Although it is difficult to be precise about the date of construction for some of the mills, it seems that

9 mills were built by 1790, and a further 13 were added in the next five years. By 1800 the total had risen to 28 and in 1810, when the last cotton mill was built in Keighley, 34 mills for spinning cotton had appeared. The attraction for local people was the profit that could be made from cotton spinning, particularly in the early years. Keighley became one of the most concentrated centres for cotton spinning in Yorkshire and some of the remains of the early buildings can still be seen. Keighley and Haworth had plenty of water power, an established textile industry, fairly easy access to the main market for cotton yarn around Blackburn and no opposition to the new industry. They also had men and women with the drive to start in the new industry and several more who recognised the business opportunities in making parts for the new machines.

Some of the early cotton spinners had no connection with the basic worsted industry of the area. For instance, Holme House Mill, Wood Mill and Goose Eye Mill, were all built by gentlemen farmers in the 1790s. Samuel Blakey, a solicitor, built Stubbin House Mill; Ingrow Corn Mill was turned over to cotton spinning by Lodge Calvert who was a joiner. However, many of the cotton spinners had previously been engaged in the worsted industry. There was a decline in the worsted trade during the 1790s, which made many of them experiment with cotton or turn over completely to the new industry. The typical business arrangement for this was a partnership, which brought together capital, and at least one partner who had some knowledge of the new machinery and factory operations.

The reasons why cotton spinning came to be established so extensively in Keighley before 1800 are fairly clear. There was a high level of demand for cotton cloth both at home and abroad. It was lighter than worsted and often cheaper than linen and could be used for a range of garments. The mechanisation of the spinning process had been established and it was well known that the early mills based on Arkwright's principles were very profitable. In the absence of any other model most of Keighley's early mills were built on the Arkwright pattern which was a mill of three stories measuring sixty feet by thirty feet. The original part of Brow End Mill at Goose Eye outside Keighley is a good example. Steam power, although used in a cotton mill at Papplewick in Nottinghamshire in 1785, was not introduced into Manchester until 1789. Its general adoption was slow and steam power was not in general use until the turn of the century when Boulton & Watt's patent expired. However, there were some local exceptions. Many of the large Leeds cotton mills had steam power, at first for pumping water back into the dam so that it could be used again by the water wheel. This method was used before rotary motion became readily available and was used at Low Mill in Keighley for a number of years. However, until 1800, apart from Low Mill, all the cotton mills in Keighley were water powered and the readily available water power sites were a key influence on the industry's location in the town.

This search for streams and rivers with a good fall was one factor that led to the building of cotton mills in the Calder valley and throughout the Craven and Yorkshire Dales. Many sites became available through the improvements

An apprentice's mistake. (See Gordon Buchanan's story, p. 161.)

in transport with the new turnpike roads and canals and consequent changes in agriculture. Corn could now be brought in cheaply from East Yorkshire so the growing of cereal crops in the West Yorkshire valleys stopped. This meant that the water powered corn mills became redundant and therefore ideal sites for the new cotton mills. The growing supply of yarn in the area meant that many hand loom weavers in Keighley and the Dales turned over to weaving cotton instead of worsted. The changes in agriculture also meant that many agricultural workers had to change over to textiles for a living and cotton weaving provided the necessary income. As every village had a corn mill, cotton spinning spread nearly everywhere with, for example, eight mills down the river Aire from Malham to Gargrave.

Another reason for the early success of the cotton industry in Yorkshire was the opposition in Lancashire to the new machines and mills. Around Blackburn and the surrounding area weaving, bleaching and calico printing were well established before 1780. More than 10,000 people were dependent on hand loom weaving for a living and large quantities of yarn were needed for the looms.[13] The problem there however, was that the larger of the new machines and mill production itself roused the opposition of the local people. So much so that in 1779 rioters ... scoured the country for several miles round Blackburn, demolishing the jennies, and with them all the carding engines, water frames, and every machine turned by water or horses. For this reason there was a reluctance to build mills and a resulting shortage of yarn which could only be met from a distance. Arkwright's mill at Birkacre near Chorley in Lancashire had been set up by a partnership including Jedediah Strutt, Samuel Need, John Cross and Thomas Walshman. This mill was destroyed in the rioting of 1779. In all ten mills were attacked with Birkacre being the largest. There appeared to be general local support for the rioters for the perpetrators were dealt with very leniently for the time. John Cross became a partner in a cotton mill in Leeds and Thomas Walshman a partner at Low Mill in Keighley. There was no opposition to mill-based cotton spinning in Yorkshire, it provided additional employment, and it was near enough to supply the Blackburn market, hungry for yarn.

After the start of Low Mill, John Greenwood built Northbrook Mill in 1782, ignoring Arkwright's patent. John Greenwood initially had problems making his machinery work efficiently as he had presumably built it himself or had it built without the help of Arkwright. The early cotton spinners were very careful about keeping the design of their spinning frames secret and also binding their employees who built the machines to secrecy. For example, Joseph Tempest, who started work for Craven, Brigg & Shackleton as their millwright at Walk Mill in 1783, was liable to pay £100 if he disclosed how their new cotton machinery was constructed or operated. After Walk Mill was adapted for cotton spinning Castle Mill and Bridgehouse Mills were built. More cotton mills were being planned, particularly as Arkwright's main patent had been overthrown in 1783. Not only in Keighley, but throughout the West Riding, construction went ahead and a number of cotton mills were built in 1784/85. These included mills in Wensleydale, Wharfedale, Ribblesdale and Calderdale.[14]

# Marriner

## New D.K. Double Knitting

# CHAPTER TWO

# Greengate Mill and the start of cotton spinning

## Greengate Mill

THE EAGERNESS OF Keighley's leading townsfolk to venture into cotton spinning in the 1780s led to a variety of business organisations. These could be single individuals or families, but more often were partnerships. It would be fascinating to know about the negotiations and planning which took place to bring together the larger partnerships such as the group who decided to build and run Greengate Mill in Keighley in 1784. The leading partner may have been Abraham Smith. He was described as a yeoman when he bought a piece of land called Dam Close in 1772 from the executors of Anthony Cooke. James Greenwood then occupied the land, while Rowland Watson was a witness to the indenture. Smith then bought the nearby West Greengate estate and four closes of land in 1775. It is doubtful if he would have had cotton spinning in mind at the time of the purchase but he went on to build or occupy Greengate House on this land on a site near the river. In 1781 Smith bought more land which had belonged to John Driver. Driver owed money to John Clapham of Utley, a wool-stapler, Joseph Blakey of Keighley, a wool stapler, Christopher Smith of Keighley, a stuff maker and Abraham Smith. Smith paid £242 for this piece of land. As Low Mill in Keighley was now completed and being used profitably for cotton spinning it would be interesting to know if Abraham Smith was planning such a use for the land he had recently acquired. It may have been that he was the moving force behind the partnership set up to build Greengate Mill for although three others contributed to the cost, it was Abraham Smith who was said to have built it.[1] Certainly the building of Low Mill with the benefit of Arkwright's support, and the public knowledge of Arkwright's financial successes, must have influenced Smith and other land-owners.

This rush into cotton spinning in the West Riding of Yorkshire after 1783, must have influenced the formation of the partnership which was to build Greengate Mill. Smith had the land but possibly did not have all the capital to build the mill and finance the first few months of operations. The partners who joined Abraham Smith were Rowland Watson, who was a solicitor and was clerk to the trustees of the Haworth Turnpike road, Joseph Blakey, a

*Greengate Mill, Keighley, 18*

*Bought of* **B. & W. MARRINER**
WORSTED SPINNERS,
And Manufacturers of Heald-Yarn.

Greengate Mill in the centre with an early extension to the left. Greengate House is on the left of the mill and the warehouse on the right.

wool stapler and John Blakey, a stuff maker. An agreement was drawn up, dated the 3 November 1784, for the four of them to commence cotton spinning. Another agreement signed on the same day brought in a fifth partner, James Greenwood the younger.[2] A part of the financial arrangements was that Smith was to be paid £43 0s. 8d. by the other partners for the 3,442¾ square yards of land on which the mill was to be built. As he held the water rights and land further up the valley he was also to be paid £210 for the firm's rights to take water from the river and through his land. As we have seen above Abraham Smith already had business dealings with Rowland Watson and Joseph Blakey. John Blakey was Joseph's brother.

The partnership division was that one third was held by Abraham Smith, one third by John Blakey and one sixth each by Rowland Watson and Joseph Blakey. As none of these men was in the cotton trade, or had any experience of building mills, constructing spinning frames or operating a factory they needed help. To obtain this help they had a second agreement with James Greenwood the younger, who was to be admitted to their partnership. The reason was that ... James Greenwood not having at present any capital to bring into stock, is ... to be employed in the said concern, because he has ... a plan in respect of other mills of a similar nature to the intended one and a genius well adapted for constructing the machines and other works to be made use of and employed in and about the said intended mill.[3]

Greenwood was to be paid thirteen shillings and six pence a week until his share of the profits amounted to a sum similar to that paid by the other partners. He was then to pay interest owing on that sum. When he had established his capital in the firm he was to be paid interest on that amount. For this he was to ... employ himself in constructing and finishing machines and other works necessary to be done in and about the said intended mill, with all best skill, knowledge and judgement and with the utmost expedition he can. He was also restricted from working for anyone else and from divulging the *secrets* of the undertaking. This need to include a partner with technical skill or employ a manager who was able to supervise the layout of the mill and assembly of the spinning machinery was common and failure to do so led to serious problems with some firms. James Greenwood the younger may have been the nephew of the James Greenwood that Abraham Smith had dealings with previously.

There was obviously every intention of making James Greenwood an equal partner with a share of the capital, for, on 9 November 1784, all five partners signed an agreement with William Sharpe for a goit to be cut through his land to bring water from the dam to the mill.[4] Greenwood's name also appears in the firm's ledger when trading started in 1785, but a year or two after that he must have left for his share of the capital was never established and he was not mentioned in any of the firm's documents again. He appears to have stayed long enough to supervise the construction of the millwork and machinery, the task for which he was originally included, at a time when his skills were rare and valuable.

There is some dispute about which James Greenwood was the partner. Hodgson wrongly uses the name John Greenwood in his account of the start of the firm. There were also at least three James Greenwoods living in the area at the time and Greenwood was a common name in the Keighley/ Haworth area. Much of the evidence points to this key partner at Greengate

Greengate House in 1963.

Title page from the first account book of Watson, Blakeys, Smith & Greenwood.

Mill being the James Greenwood who was born at Bridgehouse in Haworth in 1763. His uncle with the same name was still alive in 1784 which, would lead to his being called 'the younger'. James Greenwood's father John, was a worsted manufacturer who also owned an indigo mill and dyehouse at Bridgehouse. John Greenwood converted this mill into a cotton mill about 1783 and had as his tenants Brooks Priestley and Charles Woodiwiss. Priestley & Woodiwiss dissolved their partnership on the 19 July 1785 and Priestley then continued the firm.[5] Priestley had married James Greenwood's sister Elizabeth after her first husband William Blakey died.

Although only twenty-one in 1784, James Greenwood the younger would have had the new experience of being involved with the setting up of his father's cotton mill at Bridgehouse. This would have meant constructing the Arkwright type spinning machines from parts that were available locally. If this is correct it could have given him the knowledge and skills to put together the same spinning frames for Greengate Mill. The skill that the partners there didn't have. We don't know how long he worked at Greengate Mill, but he never became a partner. Within a year or two we do know that James Greenwood was using his knowledge and experience of the new machines to construct worsted spinning frames at Bridgehouse Mill when his father handed over the mill and other premises in 1788 or before. These early worsted frames were basically the same as the cotton spinning frames but needed skill to adapt them to the different fibre. He had become a partner in the firm of Greenwoods & Rishworth who ran Bridgehouse Mill, or possibly part of it, for worsted spinning. The partners, William Greenwood, James Greenwood and Henry Rishworth dissolved their partnership on 30 April 1789 and it was then continued by the two Greenwoods.[6] The exact date when James Greenwood and his partners started worsted spinning is not clear, but it must have been within a short while of the accepted start of mechanised worsted spinning in Yorkshire, which was 1787. The chance to start a new venture at his father's mill could have been the reason why James Greenwood left the Greengate Mill partnership about 1787 or 1788, and his background would explain his skill in developing spinning machines for both cotton and worsted.

There are no records of the expenditure involved in the construction of the buildings, water wheel and machinery at Greengate Mill. Nor are there any details of the spinning frames that were made although it is almost certain that they were water frames on the Arkwright pattern. Once the mill was running all the accounts show sales of 'cotton-twist' and it was by that name that the yarn from Arkwright's machines was known.[7] As with all other cotton spinning firms of this period the partners made their own machinery. The making of textile machinery was not new to Keighley for hand spinning wheels, probably jennies and certainly hand looms, would all be made in the area. The machines were made mainly from wood with metal being used for the rollers, gears, spindles and flyers. These could be bought roughly shaped and could be finished in the mill workshop where other parts were made. All the early cotton mills had extensive joiners' and smiths' shops, often containing models of the machinery to be copied at full scale. Low Mill, for example, employed a number of mechanics, joiners and wood turners and the first specialist firms making and repairing power-driven textile machinery did not start in Keighley until the 1790s. In the 1830s Greengate Mill had a mechanic's shop with large quantities of parts for spinning frames and models from which to work and the capability of altering or improving existing machinery continued.

The dam, goits, water wheel, mill, power transmission and machinery were built between November 1784, when the partnership agreement was signed, and October 1785 when the first sales of yarn were made. The mill measured 110 feet by 32 feet and stood for nearly two hundred years until a fire in a more modern building meant that the old mill had to be pulled down. It was a substantial, five-storey structure, built from local stone, which was easily available. The water wheel at one end was fed from a dam and goit that led from the River Worth. If the same type of wheel was retained into the next century it was a backshot wheel with the water running away under the mill and back to the river about 200 metres away. It joined the River Worth just above the weir for Walk Mill or Stell's Mill as it was sometimes called. This length of tail goit meant that maximum use could be made of the fall of water. There was a small dam near to the mill to store water and help maintain a constant level, together with a larger dam for water storage further up the valley. The first picture of the mill appears at the top of one of the firm's invoices. It shows the mill as it was about 1830, largely unchanged but with a two-storey addition. This extension to the water wheel end of the mill may have been for workshops.

The mill quickly became known as Blakey's Mill for the Blakey family were connected with it for several years. Abraham Smith retired from the business in 1790 but from 1784 until 1817 at least one and often two members of the Blakey family were in the partnership. The Blakeys were one of the leading families in Keighley at that time with several members engaged in the cotton trade. Samuel Blakey, for example, who was a solicitor, owned the Aireworth estate and built what became Aireworth Mill there in 1787 at the start of the cotton-spinning boom.[8]

## The start of cotton spinning

A surviving ledger for the period 1785 to 1790 provides a good picture of Blakeys, Smith & Watson's trading activities in those years.[9] It contains the names of both suppliers and customers, and in all cases but one, gives the name and location of the concerns with which Blakeys traded. However there may be some omissions as the date of the first transaction entered in the ledger is 9 October 1785 and is for the sale of cotton twist to Salisbury, Barrow & Co. of Chipping, a village about ten miles north of Blackburn. What is not shown is an entry prior to that date for the purchase of cotton to process into yarn. It is therefore not possible to say when the machinery in the mill started running. In addition some of the entries have been crossed out, there are entries for other items such as a horse, and doubt must exist concerning the completeness of the entries in this ledger.

The firm had its first full year of trading in 1786. Raw cotton was bought in the July from Robert Twyford, a cotton merchant in Manchester, who also supplied cotton the following year but then in exchange for yarn. The other supplier of cotton in 1786 was William Corlass of Blackburn, who was also a good customer for yarn. As the three entries for cotton purchases from the two merchants mentioned were in July, September and December, it would seem that not all cotton purchases were entered in the ledger, for the mill had already been in production for ten months.

Although some of the yarn customers occasionally made payment partly in the form of raw cotton, the main supply of cotton, as can be seen from Table 2.1 below, was usually drawn from merchants in Manchester. The city at that time was the distributing centre for raw cotton.[10] In 1788 twenty-six cotton merchants and twenty cotton dealers were in business there. These merchants became the most important source of raw cotton for Blakeys, although there were a number of times between 1786 and 1789 when raw cotton was taken from customers in part payment for yarn supplied.

| Table 2.1. Raw cotton purchases 1786–90 (£) | | | | | |
|---|---|---|---|---|---|
| Year | 1786 | 1787 | 1788 | 1789 | 1790 |
| Total Purchases | 298 | 1,580 | 705 | 2,715 | 2,047 |
| Purchases from Manchester Merchants | 170 | 1,413 | 475 | 2,510 | 2,047 |
| Number of Manchester Merchants | 1 | 5 | 2 | 1 | 1 |
| % from Manchester merchants | 51% | 92% | 11% | 80% | 100% |

Source: Purchase and Sales Ledger, 1785–90

The manufacturers who bought yarn and paid with raw cotton probably did so because of financial difficulties brought about by the decline in trade that became apparent in 1787 and 1788.[11] The East India Company sales at the end of 1787 were low, causing a surplus of cotton cloth. Early the following year one of the leading London houses failed followed by Livesey, Hargreaves & Co of Blackburn.[12] With a reduction in trade the manufacturers who were suffering from reduced sales had difficulty in paying for their warp yarn from the spinners. However, as they had stocks of cotton, which they held to supply the jenny spinners for making weft, they could use some of this to pay off their debts. In addition, as trade was reduced, any stocks of cotton they held would not be needed to the same extent. Moreover a depression in trade tended to reduce the period of credit allowed, so a payment in kind may have been one way round the problem.[13]

A good example of such dealing was that of Ridley & Crompton of Manchester. They bought £247 worth of twist in 1786, £1,494 worth in 1787 but only £56 worth in 1788. By this time they were affected by the financial difficulties and sold Blakeys £481 worth of cotton in January 1788. They soon became bankrupt and were paying only six shillings and eight pence in the pound on their debts in March 1788. Other customers that could not meet their debts were Salisbury, Barrow & Co of Chipping, John Thompson and William Corlass, both of Blackburn and Robert Smaley & Co of Darwen.

If the ledger account is an approximate record of Blakey's cotton purchases it shows a change from buying small quantities from several merchants to buying large quantities from a few merchants. In 1787, cotton to the value of £2,065 was bought from nine dealers. Six of them were Manchester merchants and the other three were Blackburn calico manufacturers who also bought Blakey's yarn. 1788 was a crisis year for the cotton trade after the rapid growth of the previous two years. There was a certain amount of over production, which is reflected in Blakey's cotton purchases. They bought only £224 worth and of this as little as £24 worth was a straight purchase from a Manchester dealer. In 1789 and 1790, the last two years for which there are records, two Manchester firms, Brocklehurst & Whittenbury and Green, Mawson & Dobson, supplied all the cotton apart from a small amount supplied by Ainsworth & Lister of Blackburn in exchange for some twist. Probably as Blakeys increased their turnover, acquired more capital and gained increased knowledge of the market, they felt confident enough to buy cotton in bulk at what they thought were favourable prices. Certainly purchases in 1790 showed a substantial increase and showed that Blakeys had weathered the earlier difficulties experienced by other firms in the cotton trade.

## Sales

The yarn spun on the water-frames at Greengate Mill was for the cheaper end of the cotton yarn market. High quality fine yarn, on which there was the highest margin of profit, could only be produced on the mule, which was not used at Greengate and was only used later by a few Keighley spinners. The country spinners, such as those in Keighley, produced the lower counts of yarn for which less skill and capital were needed. In normal trading conditions there was a large regular demand for these yarns. This came from the manufacturers who were supplying cloth to make garments for the working classes and export. Domestic servants, farm labourers and the growing number of industrial workers were turning away from linen and wool in favour of the cheaper pure cotton materials. Although this market did not yield the high profits of the fashionable trade it was more uniform.

With the mechanisation of the spinning process the cotton industry had spread out from Lancashire but the principal market for yarn was still there. Manchester in particular served as the commercial centre. The weaving firms eventually bought machine spun yarn there when they needed a variety of yarns for the different types of cloth they produced for the various markets. Initially however, the first Keighley mills produced yarn for the cotton manufacturers who organised hand-loom weaving around Blackburn and sold directly to them. This area was to remain the centre of cotton weaving for the next century. As we have seen they were denied a local source of machine spun twist following the bout of machine breaking in 1779, but the demand for yarn was not reduced. The market was considerable and the calico manufacturers or 'putters out' were prepared to buy from as far afield as Keighley to obtain the yarn needed to keep their hand loom weavers occupied. From the safety of the other side of the Pennines, Greengate Mill and other Keighley mills could easily supply these cotton manufacturers. The surviving ledger is summarised in Table 2.2. During the early years to which it relates, the majority of Blakey's customers were in the Blackburn area. Most were in Blackburn itself, but others were in the surrounding villages such as Chipping, Darwen, Leyland, Chorley, Ribchester, Church, Samlesbury, Wheelton and Brindle.

| Table 2.2. Cotton yarn sales 1785–90 (£) | | | | | | |
|---|---|---|---|---|---|---|
| | 1785[1] | 1786 | 1787 | 1788 | 1789 | 1790 |
| Total sales | 417 | 4,163 | 8,109 | 8,324 | 7,893 | 10,746 |

Source: Purchase and Sales Ledger, 1785–90

Note: 1. Entries date from 9 October 1785. All other years from 1 January

The Blackburn putter-out organised his activities in much the same way as his contemporaries in the worsted trade in Yorkshire. Cotton was put out to spin, the yarn was collected and then put out to the weavers with the cloth being returned to be finally sold for dyeing or finishing by others. Blackburn was the centre of the Lancashire cotton weaving industry with a loom an essential piece of equipment in every cottage in the town and the surrounding villages.[14] Besides weaving, the area also became the centre for calico printing and bleaching after the development of printing by rollers and the use of improved bleaching methods. It was the manufacturers of Blackburn who were the main customers for the newly available yarn from Greengate Mill as they were denied a source of locally produced yarn. One of these firms, Chippendale & Glover took half Blakey's output in the first few months of trading to the end of 1785. This firm remained a regular customer of Blakey & Co for several years and set the pattern for the concentration of sales to the Blackburn putters-out.

In 1786 sales were made to 45 customers, some of whom had been customers for yarn the previous months. Ten manufacturers took over £100 worth of yarn in 1786. Parker & Smaley of Blackburn took the largest amount, £690 worth of cotton twist. The customers that were not in or near Blackburn were firstly William Burnley of Gomersal, who took a few shillings worth of twist in 1785 and 1786. Gomersal, which is about eight miles from Leeds, was in the centre of the woollen industry, but the old cloth hall was to let in 1786 and it was suggested that it might be of interest to cotton manufacturers. William Burnley had been a partner with John Holden of Keighley until August 1784 when they had traded as stocking worsted manufacturers.[15] George & James Lowe of Stockport bought £47 worth of twist in 1786 and £26 worth in 1787. Thomas Hawksworth of Ilkley bought £51 and £50 worth in the same years. Hawksworth was described as a calico maker, stuffmaker, dealer and chapman when he was bankrupt in 1788 and had been in a partnership with Joseph Hartley, an engineer from Keighley, running a cotton mill built on Mill Ghyll in Ilkley a year or so previously. William Myers from Draughton bought a small amount of yarn and later ran a small cotton mill in that village. Stedal & Lonsdale of Kendal bought yarn in 1786 and lastly Cockshott & Lister of Addingham bought £276 worth in 1786. This last firm were cotton manufacturers who later took High Mill in Addingham for cotton spinning. There were no sales outside Lancashire after 1787 and sales to Blackburn, as a proportion of total sales, increased considerably.

The ledger from which the figures have been taken was left incomplete. Many accounts were not balanced and the last pages were left blank. Despite probable omissions the records show a rapid increase in sales from the commencement of trading. Sales of cotton twist doubled within the first two years from £4,163 in 1786 to £8,324 in 1788. The following year saw a decline, which was general throughout the industry, but 1790 brought a recovery, with total sales of £10,746.

The depression of 1787–88 seems to have been caused by overproduction in relation to demand. Competition for sales became fierce as prices were driven down and some of the more marginal firms suffered. Cotton imports were cut back and there was general concern that the new industry would suffer a setback. This recession affected the Greengate Mill concern in 1789 when sales fell below the figures for the two previous years and their customers fell away during the depression. Twenty-two customers, who together bought £2,205 worth of yarn in 1787, did not re-order in 1788. In place of those however, thirteen new names appeared in the ledger as customers in 1788 and these thirteen firms bought £3,670 worth of yarn between them. Included in the thirteen were Cardwell, Birley & Hornby and Henry Suddall, both of Blackburn. Both of these firms took over £1,000 worth of yarn. The trend was to deal with fewer firms that took larger quantities of yarn. In 1788 three customers out of the total of forty took nearly half the yarn sold.

The panic in the cotton industry in 1788 resulted in many business failures. These included Blackburn manufacturers such as Livesey, Hargreave & Co., Manchester banks and London wholesale houses.[16] As Blakeys were supplying the Blackburn weavers, who in turn were selling at the cheaper and more regular end of the market to the working classes, the depression did not affect them as much as it did the muslin manufacturers. A possible reason for the apparent contradiction that sales of yarn from Greengate Mill fell in the year that trade generally improved, 1789, could be that the lower prices of cheap cottons caused by the glut of the previous year had led to a temporary satisfaction of demand. A further reason was that the muslin manufacturers started to devote more of their time to the production of cheaper materials in 1789 and so affected the sale of calicoes.

Both total sales and the number of customers fell in 1789 but some of these customers were taking large quantities of yarn. Turner & Son of Blackburn, who had bought a small amount of twist in 1786, bought £543 worth. Joshua Fielden & Son of Blackburn, who had bought large amounts in the two previous years, did so again, while Henry Suddall, also of Blackburn, who had taken an eighth of the mill's output in 1788 increased his share to a fifth in 1789. The large sales made to William Corlass and Cardwell, Birley & Hornby in 1788 were not repeated. Corlass owed £232 at the end of 1788 and could only pay off £147 the next year. The balance was allowed as discount, presumably because of his previous good orders.

The year 1790 was the last covered by the ledger. Sales rose to £10,746, a quarter of which was accounted for by one firm, that of Henry Suddall of Blackburn. He came from a Lancashire family, which had prospered over the years with the growth of the cotton industry. Coming originally from farming stock, the family took to trade as chapmen in the seventeenth century and became merchants and eventually cotton manufacturers in the eighteenth. By 1800 Henry Suddall was one of the most affluent men in the area. It was said that he was the most influential merchant and manufacturer in Blackburn with great deference shown to him by the workpeople there. He had a country estate at Mellor and was reputed to be a millionaire, but his success did not last for he was bankrupt in 1827.[17]

Sales of cotton yarn to Lancashire firms did continue however, as John Turner of Colne was a customer until the end of 1799. He had been a shopkeeper and calico manufacturer but was bankrupt and had to assign his estate to Watson, Blakeys & Marriner as well as two other firms.[18]

A valuable customer, such as Suddall, was an indication of the extent to which Blakeys had penetrated the cotton yarn market. The size and importance of their Blackburn customers show the success they had in building up trade with some of the leading cotton manufacturers. Cardwell, Birley & Hornby were another example. Although this firm had a spinning mill at Scorton near Garstang, they needed additional supplies of yarn to stock their ware-house at Clayton Street in Blackburn. There they stored yarn and conducted their business as putters-out to hand loom weavers. These and other Blackburn manufacturers continued to prosper despite setbacks to trade such as the depression of 1788 and later the French wars. The Suddalls and Fieldens had moved out of the town to country estates by the 1790s. Peel, Yates & Co, who built a calico printing works in Bury about 1770, became customers of Greengate Mill in 1790 and went on to become one of the largest firms in the area.

The attic room in the old mill.

No comparable sales accounts survive for any of the other ten or so cotton mills in the Keighley area, which had been built by 1790, so it is impossible to know where their yarn was sold. Lancashire men built Low Mill so it is likely that yarn from there was taken to Lancashire to be woven. When Ponden Mill was built in 1791 by Robert Heaton, who had been a worsted manufacturer, it was said that the direction of his trade changed from the road to Halifax to the road to Colne and then to Blackburn. It would seem likely that much if not all the cotton yarn spun in the early Keighley mills went to the Lancashire weaving area around Blackburn. However, some time during the 1790s cotton weaving started in West Yorkshire and grew to challenge the traditional worsted industry. The local hand loom weavers changed from weaving worsted to weaving calico and throughout the region thousands of cotton pieces were woven each week and sent to Manchester. That, however, was the second phase of development for the firm which ran Greengate Mill.

## Profits

Unfortunately there are no records for expenditure on wages or other costs for this early period and so it is not possible to ascertain whether the firm made a profit or loss. However, judging by the way more and more cotton-spinning mills were being built in Keighley, it would seem likely that cotton spinning was, at that time, a profitable venture. Twenty-eight mills were built between 1780 and 1800 when steam power became more readily available.

*Right*:
Lower yard at Greengate Mill.

*Below, top*:
Greengate Mill in 1983.

*Below, bottom*:
Greengate Mill in the 1930s.

Furthermore Blakeys continued to spin cotton until 1817 and Marriners even possibly continued after that time in a limited way for a few more years. A simple subtraction of raw material costs from yarn sales for the years from 1786 to 1790 gives some indication of the value added by using the water twist frame for spinning.

| Table 2.3 | | | | | |
|---|---|---|---|---|---|
| Year | 1786 | 1787 | 1788 | 1789 | 1790 |
| Yarn sales | £4,163 | £8,109 | £8,324 | £7,893 | £10,746 |
| Cotton purchased | £260 | £2,065 | £224 | £1,054 | £3,709 |
| Difference | £3,903 | £6,044 | £8,100 | £6,839 | £7,037 |

Source: Purchase and Sales Ledger 1785–90

This first five or six year period saw the firm of & Watson, Blakeys & Smith well established. They were buying from the specialist Manchester cotton merchants in increasing quantities instead of the small dealers. Sales had increased dramatically from 1785 to 1790, by which time they were supplying some of the leading cotton manufacturers in the Blackburn area, which was the centre of the cotton weaving trade in the country. Regular customers had been gained at a time of rising competition and Greengate Mill was now in the centre of increasing number of similar mills all devoted to cotton spinning.

# CHAPTER THREE

# *From cotton to worsted*

---

THE YEARS from 1790 to 1817 saw changes in the activities and ownership of Greengate Mill. Cotton spinning continued at the mill but the warehouse and other sections became increasingly important when the weaving of cotton cloth started. Large numbers of hand loom weavers were employed to weave calico pieces. They were self-employed and lived some distance from the mill. Yarn had to be given out and then cloth taken in from the weavers before it was sent to Manchester. This continued for several years and added a new dimension to the firm's sales. Weaving cotton was a new industry for the area but appeared to be an easy transition for the hand loom weavers from the weaving of worsted. They no longer had to weave hand-spun worsted yarn but machine-spun cotton yarn. The selling of cloth instead of yarn again meant a different direction for the work of Blakeys & Marriner. Manchester took over from Blackburn as the focus for their sales. This continued until 1817, but, by then, cotton weaving had became unprofitable for Blakeys and like most local manufacturers their spinning mill turned to worsted, although this was accompanied by a change in ownership. By that time cotton spinning machinery had been successfully adapted to spin worsted yarn on a commercial scale and after 1817 Greengate Mill started to produce worsted yarn instead of cotton. These changes, which eventually affected all the Keighley cotton spinning firms, were accompanied by several changes in the partnership at Greengate Mill and resulted in the Marriner family gaining complete control.

The year 1790 marked the dividing point between the early stages of the organisation of the cotton trade in Britain and its later development.[1] The shortage of yarn, which for so long hindered the development of weaving, had been overcome and spinning mills of all types had been built. The inventions of Hargreaves, Arkwright and Crompton had been widely adopted, and by increasing the supply of yarn, made possible the large scale production of all types of cotton cloth. In Yorkshire a variety of cotton mills were built with large steam powered mills in Leeds and Sheffield, horse mills in some places but mainly water powered mills. Arkwright type mills sprang up throughout the Yorkshire Dales while Crompton's mule was widely used in Calderdale. This mechanisation of spinning, and the huge rise in the production of cotton yarn, resulted in a boom in cotton weaving but this was still basically a cottage industry. Hand looms were cheap to make and provided a living for thousands of people in the locality. Areas of Bradford such as

Little and Great Horton were given over to cotton weaving and the weekly coach that carried the local manufacturers to Manchester was known as the 'Calico Coach'.[2] In Settle it was said that ... the sound of the hand loom might be heard in every village in the district, and in almost every street.[3]

The two areas of demand for cotton goods, the home and foreign markets, grew rapidly but suffered several changes of fortune. The early 1790s were boom years, for despite the outbreak of war with France in 1793, it was possible to shift trade from Europe to America. During the following twenty years, however, there occurred a series of swings in trade that, although there were good years, produced many difficulties for both spinners and manufacturers. The French wars, with blockades and volatile markets, led to a number of bankruptcies, declining profits and firms going out of the cotton trade altogether. These trading difficulties, together with the development of larger, steam-powered mills in Lancashire after 1800, eventually caused serious problems throughout much of West Yorkshire. The demand for the coarser yarns, in which the Keighley firms specialised, kept up better than that for fine yarns. Despite this they also suffered declining profits with increased competition. This again resulted in firms changing hands, an increased rate of bankruptcy, and soon afterwards most Keighley mills ceased to spin cotton as new business opportunities rose through the mechanisation of worsted spinning.

## Keighley

Despite the problems, the eagerness to build mills for spinning cotton in Keighley continued for another twenty years after 1790 until the last cotton mill to be built, Beckstones Mill, was constructed in 1810. Twenty-five new cotton mills were built after 1790 compared with nine between 1780 and 1790. The exact dates when each mill was built are not always easy to establish, but this concentration of cotton mills was one of the most extensive in the country. Until 1800 mills were built on the River Worth and North Beck, but when steam power became readily available after that time other sites could be used.

When Beckstones Mill was built existing mills were gradually being changed over to spin worsted. Hodgson instances many cotton spinning firms which were in serious difficulties after 1815. William Wilkinson of Castle Mill became bankrupt in 1815 and although his son, a timber merchant and ironmonger, took over the firm, he too was bankrupt within a few years. A similar fate befell Thomas Corlass who had built Hope Mill on land next to Greengate Mill in 1800.

> For several years Mr Corlass was engaged at this mill in spinning cotton, but, like the majority of cotton spinners in this parish, he found it anything but a paying concern. Being vexed and agitated by the unfavourable state of the markets, he one morning went to the engine tenter and ordered him to rake out the fire and stop the engine; and this being done, he from that time ceased to be a cotton spinner.[4]

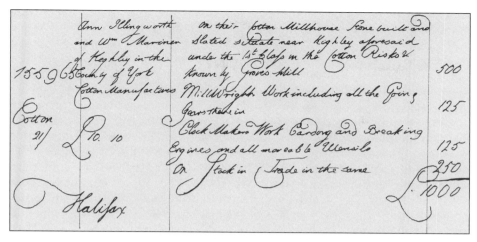

1797 Insurance for Grove Mill owned by Ann Illingworth and William Marriner.

Hodgson also mentions William Illingworth of Grove Mill in similar vein. William Marriner had been a partner with Ann Illingworth and later her two sons, William and David, until his death in 1809. William Marriner's one-third share then passed to his two sons. One of them, Benjamin Marriner, was a working partner at Grove Mill, helping to buy and sell cotton, but Illingworths later ran the mill themselves only to encounter difficulties.

Mr Illingworth, like the majority of those who in this neighbourhood were engaged in the cotton trade, did not succeed in saving money, but ultimately came to grief. He gave up business in 1819.[5]

The population of Keighley parish rose from 5,745 in 1801 to 6,864 in 1811 and 9,223 in 1821. During that time the worsted trade re-established itself as the dominant industry. More mills were built and the the later ones were all for spinning worsted yarns. It is not always possible to be completely accurate about the total number of mills in existence at any one time or about the dates when they changed over to spinning worsted from cotton. Many of the early mills were about the size of a few cottages. Some went out of existence when the size of machinery increased and they could no longer compete with their larger neighbours. If they were in the right location and had access to a good water supply they were sometimes rebuilt or new buildings were added. The introduction of steam power meant that mills could be built away from the Worth and North Beck. Hope Mill and Low Bridge Mill, both built in 1800, were originally cotton mills, but were steam powered. The balance between water and steam then started to change, but it took nearly the rest of the century for waterpower to be reduced to an insignificant level. Other factors had an influence. Fire was always a hazard, but if the firm was insured or had enough capital a mill was usually rebuilt. Even in 1833 when mill owners had to give details to the Factory Enquiry Commissioners some mill owners did not know when their mill was built. Hodgson, in 1879, with his knowledge of the industry and local help, was not able to say which was the first mill built for worsted spinning in Keighley.

## Cotton purchases

After 1790 few records remain relating to cotton purchases by the Greengate Mill concern. However, a notebook exists, detailing frequent visits to Manchester from 1814 with many transactions relating to cotton. It is likely that the book belonged to Benjamin Marriner and the entries relate to his work as a partner with the Illingworths at Grove Mill, not Greengate Mill, for Benjamin and William inherited this one-third partnership from their father. Later entries in the notebook relate to land at Frizinghall near Bradford, which was owned by Benjamin Marriner's wife, which again suggests again that this was his notebook. Mention is made of a dispute regarding the water supply to Emmott's mill downstream from Grove Mill, which would have been Ingrow Mill. Emmotts had changed over from cotton spinning to worsted in November 1811 and their new machinery was more efficient and did not require as much power from the water wheel as the old cotton frames. Although the information relates to a different firm it is useful in that it has details of cotton purchases. In addition it shows that Benjamin, as the elder brother and only about twenty years old, was very much involved in business transactions, travelled frequently and was well prepared to take over the running of Greengate Mill with the help of his younger brother. The partnership at Grove Mill also dealt with some of the same firms in Manchester as Blakeys. James Gibson, for instance, must have had calico pieces from both firms in his warehouse at the same time.

During frequent visits to Manchester between December 1814 and June 1817, Benjamin jotted down some brief details of purchases. Cotton was bought in 1814 from such Manchester merchants as Brierley & Harrison, Mr Ward of Half Moon Court and John Hurst. The types bought were Cuba, Brazil and Marahan. In January of the next year he bought Demarara from William Tiplady, Carthagena and Marahan from John Hurst and Prime Brazil from John Robinson. In March he was buying Sea Island and Bahamas cotton. These visits were made, not only for buying but also for selling. He bought cotton only from merchants and generally he paid for it on a subsequent visit with an adjustment made for weight discrepancies when the cotton reached Keighley.

During 1815 and 1816 the firm bought a range of raw cotton from John Hurst & Co of 3 Bank Street, William Tiplady of 6 Swan Court, Joseph Robinson of Cromford Court, Scholes & Kirk of 10 New Market Street and William Loundes of 20 New Cannon Street. At times Demarara or Brazil long staple cotton featured. This was used for spinning twist for warps, but in the same order could be Orleans, which was used for weft. Generally the cotton was of the type to be used for making warps, which would fit with the machinery in the mill, while weft was obtained as yarn from other spinners.[6]

## Cotton weaving

The significant advantage of nearly all the larger Keighley cotton mills was that when worsted spinning became more profitable they could be converted to spin worsted at very little additional expense. Several Keighley worsted manufacturers had gone into cotton spinning as an additional enterprise but retained their worsted interests. Others continued as before, but changes were forced on them when machine spun worsted became available. However, initially it was cotton weaving which grew in importance, but which left little trace behind because it was based on the hand loom and the individual efforts of thousands of weavers in the towns, villages, hamlets and farms, not only around Keighley, but also much further afield in the Craven Dales. Although specially designed weavers cottages were built in parts of Yorkshire, most weavers, men and women, worked at looms set up in living rooms, bedrooms or cellars. In the country, or where there was space, out-houses or other buildings might have been used. Certainly the addresses of Marriner's worsted weavers, slightly after this period, are streets of small terrace houses. Unlike worsted weaving, the weaving of cotton on a hand loom was easier in damp conditions such as a cellar or basement.

As we have seen earlier there was already a well-established system for organising the weaving of worsted cloth in the areas away from the towns. Transport by cart or canal was available together with a network of agents and even shops, which would give out yarn to weavers. This continued until worsted power-loom weaving was introduced gradually from the mid-1830s. However, the rise of the cotton industry persuaded many hand loom weavers to change to weaving cotton and they were joined by many displaced farm workers. The growth of cotton weaving in the area is highlighted by an extract from *Rees' Cyclopaedia* for 1808.

> The lightness as well as the cheapness of the calico has rendered it a chief article of dress amongst all classes of people, and annihilated the manufacture of many of the lighter kinds of woollen and worsted stuffs formerly so much in demand. The trade of Halifax and the surrounding country, which consisted almost wholly in such stuffs, has gone entirely into decay and been replaced by the manufacture of calicoes and other cotton goods, and such are the quantities now manufactured, more especially in the country around Colne and thence to Bradford, that from 16 to 20,000 pieces are brought weekly to the Manchester market.

The Marriner papers include three weavers' account books. The first covers the period from 1804 to 1814 with an inexplicable gap of a few years in between. The relevance of this first account is that it deals with the weaving of calicoes and the weavers are all well away from Keighley. However, it is possible that cotton weaving started before 1804 and went on after 1814. In addition there may have been other ledgers, which have not survived. The names of the men and women listed in this first book are usually followed by a place name, presumably where they lived and worked. Several clusters can be identified with an interesting pattern, which suggests that yarn was distributed by canal to two centres at Gargrave and Marton. There is no other evidence to substantiate this, but a large number of the weavers listed lived at or near these centres with others also living along the route of the Leeds and Liverpool Canal.

Gargrave was very much a cotton village with three mills by 1800. Twenty of the hand loom weavers lived there, another twenty-four lived further up the valley at Airton and there were others at Malham, Bellbusk, Coniston Cold and Eshton. What is surprising is that all these villages also had cotton mills. Other weavers within easy reach of Gargrave worked at Cracoe, Rilston and Hetton, where there were small mills at this time. Transport from the canal warehouses at Skipton or Gargrave was also easy into the Wharfe Valley, where weavers at Coniston, Grassington, Burnsall and Thorpe worked for Blakeys. Here again there were nearby cotton mills at Kettlewell, Grassington, Linton and Hartlington.

East and West Marton, further to the west on the canal, had a small cotton mill run by a local publican called John Bond. His name occurs several times in the ledger and twenty-five of the weavers worked in Marton with others at Broughton and Newton, which are nearby. Bond may have been a local agent for his name is scrawled across several pages. Further along the canal other weavers worked at Thornton, Earby and Fence near Padiham in Lancashire.

## Machinery used at Greengate Mill

The machinery used at the mill appeared to change little in the later years of cotton spinning. Indeed, according to the stock book, the value of the machinery changed hardly at all between 1808 and 1815. However, in 1816, at a time when many cotton spinning firms were failing in Keighley, and the year before the Marriner brothers gained full control of the firm, the value of the machinery was written down quite substantially.

| | Spinning frames | Roving frames | Drawing frames | Goliaths | Fine cards | Breaker cards |
|---|---|---|---|---|---|---|
| **Table 3.1. Value of machinery at Greengate Mill, taken from stockbook (£)** | | | | | | |
| 1808 | 1,440 | 112 | 36 | 100 | 275 | 220 |
| 1815 | 1,440 | 180 | 100 | 100 | 270 | 220 |
| 1816 | 792 | 180 | 50 | 40 | 50 | 45 |

Lack of financial data and knowledge of their accounting procedures make it impossible to say anything about the firm's policy for making financial allowances for the depreciation of machinery. The valuation of the preparing and spinning machinery for the period to 1815 shows that there was no acknowledgement of the need for a reserve fund as the machinery apparently did not depreciate in value. This attitude to the accounting procedure for capital equipment was typical of the time. It was usual to accept items of capital expenditure as being part of the current working of the enterprise.

The increase in the value of the four drawing frames mentioned above was probably due to an improvement to them which occurred in 1814 and which would have been paid for at the time.

## Labour

Most workers in the new cotton mills were children. The employers tried to bring together large numbers of them to operate the new machines on a two-shift system so that the mills could run 24 hours a day. If they were local, a bell would be used to summon them to work. If they were apprentices, the apprentice house would be near the mill. For the children, and even the adults, the tasks they had to undertake were new. It is not clear where the first mill children in Keighley came from. There are a number of examples in Yorkshire where children came from parishes in London and other towns as parish apprentices to work in the new mills. The parishes were able to reduce the number of destitute or orphaned children they were responsible for and at the same time satisfy themselves that the children were being started in an apprenticeship. The mill-owners had a supply of cheap labour as they didn't have to pay their apprentices but did have to provide accommodation, food, clothing and supervision. Clayton & Walshman from Keighley, built cottages near their new mill at Langcliffe near Settle and advertised in 1787 for large families to live there as the children could be employed.[7] However, Keighley and the surrounding hamlets could probably supply the numbers of children required as the early mills were strung out for several miles along the Worth and North Beck and no examples of the use of imported apprentice children have been found. The families of the local hand-combers and hand loom weavers were probably sufficient to supply the early mills.

The treatment of children in the new factories and the long hours they worked, some at night, brought a movement to control the situation. This led to an Act in 1802 'for the preservation of the health and morals of apprentices and others, employed in cotton and other mills, and cotton and other factories'. The mill owners, of course, opposed this legislation. Early in February 1802 a meeting was held in Leeds to oppose the new Act which related to mills and factories within Great Britain and Ireland which employed three or more apprentices or twenty or more other persons. The Act stated that rooms in the mills had to be whitewashed twice a year and windows or openings must be provided for ventilation. Apprentices had to be given two new suits of clothing each year, the dormitories for boys and girls had to be separate and not more than two apprentices should sleep in the same bed. The main feature of the Act was that the working hours of apprentices were restricted to twelve between the hours of six in the morning and nine at night. Additional time could be taken for meals but night working was forbidden after the 1 June 1803. Apprentices had to attend Sunday school each Sunday and attend church or chapel at least one Sunday in each month. To supervise this legislation the justices in each county had to appoint two people unconnected with the mills to visit them. One of the visitors had to be a justice of the peace and the other a clergyman of the Established Church. Initially however, mill-owners had to register their mills and the numbers of apprentices and other people they employed. Many mill-owners were either unaware of their obligation to do this or ignored the legislation.

On the 8 January 1803 the registration process started for Keighley with Illingworths & Marriner being the first to register with Groves Mill. A further ten were registered on 29 January including Greengate Mill which was then run by Watson, Blakey, Marriner & Ellis.[8] The Act, with its restrictions on the hours and conditions of the mill workers, resulted in a meeting of cotton mill owners in the Keighley area on the 9 February to consider a response and they formed a committee of fifteen members to oppose it. The name and place of the mill or mills they ran have been added.

| | |
|---|---|
| William Willett | Castlefield Mill, Bingley |
| Peter Garforth | High Mill, Skipton |
| John Greenwood | various mills, Keighley |
| Lister Ellis | Greengate Mill and others |
| William Ellis | Greengate Mill and others |
| John Sidgwick | High Mill, Skipton |
| George Merryweather | Greenholme Mill, Burley-in-Wharfedale |
| James Ross | Griffe Mill, Stanbury |
| Hill Barker | Upper Mill, Morton |
| Robert Heaton | Ponden Mill, Stanbury |
| Jonathan Barker | Upper Mill, Morton |
| Mr Hollings | Griffe Mill, Stanbury |
| Thomas Leach | Dalton Mill, Keighley |
| Timothy Horsfall | Goit Stock Mill, Harden, Bingley |

The main resolutions of the meeting were:

That it is the unanimous opinion of this meeting that the Act of Parliament respecting apprentices and others employed in cotton and woollen factories will in its effect be highly injurous to the spinners of cotton and proprietors of mills.

That a committee be appointed to obtain a repeal or modification of the said Act, any five of whom shall be competent to act with, or add to their number.

That such committee consist of the following gentlemen – Mr W M Willett, Mr Clayton, Mr Peter Garforth Jnr, Mr John Greenwood, Mr Lister Ellis, Mr William Ellis, Mr Sidgwick, Mr George Merryweather, Mr Ross, Mr Barker, Mr Robert Heaton, Mr Jonathan Barker, Mr Hollings, Mr Thomas Leach and Mr Horsfall.

That a subscription be entered into to carry the above resolution into effect and the amount of several subscriptions paid into the hands of Messrs Greenwood and Ellis, Keighley.

That the petition to the House of Commons (now read) for leave to bring in a Bill for the repeal or modification of the said Act is approved.

That the chairman to be requested to transmit the petition, when signed, to the Hon. Henry Lascelles, one of the representatives of this county, desiring him to present the same.

That a correspondence be entered into with the committee of the cotton trade in Manchester.[9]

There is no evidence that this committee had any effect and night working for children was soon phased out.

## Keighley machine makers

The mill mechanic at Greengate Mill from 1797 to 1800 was Berry Smith. When he left to work for himself most of his work was the repair of machinery for the cotton spinners in the town and elsewhere. Smith's experience at Greengate would have been useful for this, as indeed, would his experience prior to 1797 when he was apprenticed to William Carr who came to make spinning frames in Keighley. Berry Smith was typical of many Keighley textile machine makers who served an apprenticeship in the town and later went on to found their own firms. However, two of the foremost machine makers came from outside the town, William Carr came from Chipping in Lancashire, where he had managed a mill, and Richard Hattersley from Sheffield. Hattersley, strictly speaking, was not originally a machine maker, but a whitesmith, but most of his early work in Keighley was in supplying rollers, spindles, flyers and other parts for textile machines which others manufactured. He came from Eccleshall near Sheffield where a large cotton mill had been built by 1788. In 1789 he started business at Stubbing House Mill which had been built in 1787 by Samuel Blakey and used for cotton spinning and the making of metal screws by Cawood, Wright & Binns. In July 1789 Cawood left and Rowland Watson who was a partner at Greengate Mill joined the other partners. Hattersley started in a small way, but in 1793 became a partner with Thomas Binns that lasted until Binn's death in 1810. He supplied parts to most of the machine makers in Keighley and also to the textile firms, who constructed their own machines or needed to repair or up-date existing spinning frames. He did not make complete machines himself until about 1818. In 1801 Richard Hattersley supplied Blakeys at Greengate Mill with metal parts used in making spinning frames. The items were:

'February 18th – to rollers £4.4.0

April 23rd – 10 dozen spindles and flyers 24 shillings'

Richard Hattersley's sons, despite various setbacks, went on to establish other branches and also started worsted manufacturing. George Hattersley, and his son, R L Hattersley later achieved great success making power looms

Bill head from Richard Hattersley & Sons.

and ... laid the foundation of the greatest fortune that was ever acquired by any one man residing in the town of Keighley.

William Carr did not establish the same dynasty of machine makers as Richard Hattersley. His sons carried on the trade for some years but diversified out of textile machinery. However, during his working life, William Carr supplied cotton spinners in Keighley and other parts of Yorkshire. He bought components from Richard Hattersley to made spinning frames and eventually throstles. Some of the first items he bought about 1794 were for Jonathon Bracken at Jowler Mill in the Luddenden Valley and Baynes, Barker, Spencers & Co. of Millholme Mill at Embsay outside Skipton. There is an account that the first throstle he made was supplied to Blakeys at Greengate Mill in 1798. Carr was important in that he trained textile engineers such as Berry Smith who in turn trained others.

The cotton-spinning boom in Keighley in the 1780s and 1790s had attracted William Carr and Richard Hattersley to the town. Many of the flourishing textile engineering firms of later years, and also machine tool firms, can be linked with these and more numerous local men who trained as mill mechanics or were apprenticed to the towns textile engineering firms. The growing textile industry in the area provided ample business opportunities and there appeared to be a climate of support for enterprising men who left their masters and set up on their own.[10]

The need for competent mill mechanics who could build new machines as well as maintain existing ones continued for many years. In 1810 Blakeys bought brass and ironwork valued at £69 from George Richardson who had previously been a partner with William Carr. At the end of the same year a new spinning frame at a cost of £80 had been added and in 1817, when the Blakeys sold out to the Marriner brothers, John Blakey asked to be allowed to have a roving frame which still had to be completed in the mill workshop.

Greengate mill was extended during the cotton spinning period from 1784 to 1817 and the dam was enlarged in the early 1800s. Some idea of the capital of the firm may be judged by the valuation placed on it for the insurance issued by the Globe Insurance in 1813. This was made out to John and Thomas

Blakey and Ann Marriner as her husband had died in 1809. The mill, equipment and stock were insured for the following amounts:[11]

|  | £ |
| --- | --- |
| 5 storey cotton mill with 1,500 sq. yards of flooring | 1,000 |
| Water wheel and millwright's gear | 400 |
| Clockmaker's work, carding and breaking engines | 1,000 |
| Separate warehouse | 200 |
| Stock in warehouse | 800 |
| **Total = 3,400** | |

There were certain exclusion clauses relating to the processing of cotton in rooms where there were stoves, open lamps or candles. These formed a fire risk on account of the dust, which was caused by batting or picking cotton wool.

## Sales of cotton cloth

Details of the volume of cotton cloth made up and sold by the partners at Greengate Mill are sparse. At the end of 1810 there was an entry in the stock book for:

1,253 calicoes          13/–          £814.9.0

However, this would be stock on hand rather than sales but it does indicate a good level of activity as 1809 and 1810 were boom years for the export of cotton yarn and cloth. The move into manufacturing was not uncommon in Keighley. William & John Haggas started to weave cotton pieces after 1801 when they took Higher Providence Mill for cotton spinning. Similarly, Lodge Calvert had woven cotton pieces at Ingrow before 1808. Haggas Brothers and Lodge Calvert were also customers of Greengate Mill for they both bought warps from Greengate during 1815. Both these firms were on the list of six cotton manufacturers who attended the Manchester cotton goods market from Keighley in 1814. The others who attended were John Ellison, William Roper & Son and William Wilkinson & Son.[12]

The weaving of cotton pieces by Blakeys continued and in 1813 there was mention of 'Calicoes', 'Prints', 'Fents' and 'warp and weft' and in the following year 'warp and weft in weavers hands'. From entries in Benjamin Marriner's notebook relating to Grove Mill it would seem that the firm there was spinning mainly warp yarn so they had to buy weft or exchange their warps for weft. For instance on 28 May 1816 he made the following entry ... Bartered with Jno. Sutcliffe & Son for 2 skeps No. 30 weft to 2/4½ to be paid for in warps to be sent to James Stead, Sizer, North Bridge, Halifax.

At the end of 1816, the last year for which stock records were made before the mill went over to worsted spinning, they again had warp and weft with the weavers, with lengths of cloth in the warehouse described as handkerchiefs, prints, rough shirting and strong calicoes.

Blakeys sold some of their cotton cloth through a Manchester agent called

Annie Lund's experiences as a mill girl in the 1930s. (See p. 164.)

James Gibson. He was paid 1d in the pound commission and also a porterage charge of one shilling and six pence per cent. Regular visits were made to see Gibson. On the visits it was noted what stocks the agent had in his warehouse. Money Gibson had taken from sales during the previous period was collected and then often used to pay the cotton merchants for the raw cotton sent to Keighley. There is a small piece of paper dated December 1814, which gives details of stock in Gibson's warehouse:

| 12th Light Supers | 382 | Heavy | 83 |
|---|---|---|---|
| 6th Sent | 96 | | 96 |
| | 478 | | 179 |

A large part of the yarn produced at Greengate Mill must have gone into making cloth because Gibson held stock valued at £2,118 in April 1816. From the little information available on prices it would seem that they fell from about fifteen shillings a piece in 1814 to around twelve shillings at the end of 1816.

## Profits

There are only a few brief details about profits during this period. William Marriner, who had a one-third share in the partnership at this time, noted that he received the following sums as profits:

| 1802 | £853 2s. 0d. | The total profit for the firm | £2,559 6s. 0d. |
|---|---|---|---|
| 1803 | £97 18s. 0d. | would therefore be: | −£293 14s. 0d. |
| 1804 | £437 18s. 0d. | | £1,313 14s. 0d. |

The amount for 1802 is not surprising, as that was a most prosperous year for cotton spinners. William Marriner was also a partner at Grove Mill from which he also received £70 profit but the year was not specified.

The good years did not last however, for despite the move into cotton weaving the cotton trade eventually became unprofitable. Benjamin Marriner later entered in his diary that their partnership with the Illingworths at Grove Mill had lost £200 in 1813 and £400 in 1814. As seen already losses were not unusual at that time. Robert Heaton of Ponden Mill, further up the valley, lost £569 between 1811 to 1813.

The situation after 1815 is not clear. There was the downward valuation of the cotton preparing and spinning machinery in 1816, which followed the losses of the previous years. The young Marriner brothers had an independent business, which may have been profitable, as it was a period of prosperity for the worsted trade. They had also inherited £2,110 from their father when he died in 1809. He had previously been able to buy the one-sixth share from Lister Ellis in 1805, which gave the family a half share in the firm. When Thomas Blakey died these factors possibly influenced the other partner to sell his share in an apparently declining firm to Benjamin and William Marriner who had the experience, and probably the capital, to change it over to worsted spinning and manufacturing. It is not known how the capital for the purchase of the half of the firm held by Thomas and John Blakey was raised. The price paid, however, gave the concern a valuation of £4,900, which included £2,365 for stock in trade and machinery.

# CHAPTER FOUR

# The Marriner family takes control

THE TRANSFER OF OWNERSHIP of the shares of the original partners can be seen in Table 4.1. James Greenwood never became a partner as planned but went on to run Bridgehouse and other mills. Abraham Smith's one-third share was left to his niece Ann Flesher. Her mother and father, Margaret Smith and Hugh Flesher lived at Howden Gate near Silsden and Ann had looked after her uncle, as he was not married. He had lived at Greengate House close to the mill and retired in 1790. Ann Flesher married William Marriner in 1792 and notes on a scrap of paper, presumably written by one of his relatives, record that ... It was mentioned in the paper last week that your cousin Wm Marriner was married to Miss Fletcher (sic) with a fortune of Five Thousand Pounds. The witnesses to the marriage were David and William Illingworth, William Marriner's partners at Grove Mill.

William Marriner was born in Settle in 1757 and was the only child of Benjamin and Jane Marriner. Benjamin was described as a yeoman in contemporary records and his relatives appear to have been landowners and farmers in the Settle – Kirkby Lonsdale area. There was a family interest in quarrying, for in 1797 some slate quarries at Ingleton were for sale and had been occupied by his cousin, also William Marriner.[1] However, William was apprenticed to William Sinclair, a linen draper of Skipton, at the age of nineteen. The term of his apprenticeship was four years from 1776, during which time Sinclair was to provide William Marriner with all his needs except clothing and wages. The indenture followed the usual pattern of the time with clauses forbidding the apprentice such things as playing at cards or dice, visiting alehouses and marriage. (See William Marriner's Apprenticeship Indenture, overleaf.)

This apprenticeship as a draper was most useful to William Marriner for it gave him experience of certain aspects of the cotton trade which were to be of value later. It was an apprenticeship, which several other men turned to their advantage in the cotton trade.[2] David Dale, who with help from Richard Arkwright, founded New Lanark mills in Scotland, Robert Owen who followed him and Samuel Oldknow, another Arkwright partner, were all apprenticed to drapers before going on to establish fortunes in the cotton trade. Similarly in Keighley, Thomas Waterhouse, who took room and power in Greengate Mill in 1837, was a draper and cotton manufacturer at the same time from 1810.

The training in a draper's shop which many cotton manufacturers and

## William Marriner's apprenticeship indenture

This Indenture made the twenty-sixth day of October in the seventeenth year of the reign of our sovereign lord King George the third and in the year of our Lord Christ One Thousand Seven Hundred and Seventy-Six between Benjamin Marriner of Settle in Craven in the County of York, Yeoman, of the first part, William Marriner, son of the said Benjamin Marriner, of the second part and William Sinclair of Skipton in Craven aforesaid linen draper of the third part. Witnesseth that the said William Marriner hath of his own free and voluntary will and with the consent of his said father put, placed and bound himself apprentice to the said William Sinclair to learn the said trade, mastery or occupation of a linen draper which the said William Sinclair now useth, And with him as an apprentice to dwell, continue and serve, from the day of the date hereof, unto the full end and term of four years from thence next ensuing and fully to be completed and ended during all which term of four years the said apprentice his said master shall well and faithfully serve his secrets, keep his lawful commands, gladly do and obey. Hurt to his said master he shall not do, nor wilfully suffer to be done by others but of the same to the utmost of his power shall forthwith give notice to his said master. The goods of his said master he shall not embezzle or waste nor them lend without his consent to any. At cards, dice or any other unlawful games he shall not play. Taverns or alehouses he shall not frequent; fornication he shall not commit; matrimony he shall not contract; from the service of his said master he shall not at any time depart or absent himself without his said master's leave; but in all things as a good and faithful apprentice shall and will demean and behave himself towards his said master and all his family during the said term. And the said William Sinclair for himself, his executors, administrators and assignees in consideration as aforesaid, and of five shillings of lawful money of Great Britain to him in hand, paid by the said William Marriner covenanteth and agreeth to and with the said Benjamin Marriner, his executors, administrators and assignees by these presents that he the said William Sinclair shall well and sufficiently teach and instruct, or cause to be well and sufficiently taught and instructed, to his said apprentice the trade, mystery or occupation of Linen Draper which the said William Sinclair knoweth after the best way and manner he can, and shall and will also find and allow to his said apprentice sufficient and enough meat, drink, washing and lodging and all other necessaries fit and convenient for such an apprentice (linen and wearing apparel only accepted) during the term aforesaid in witness whereof the parties above said have hereto interchangeably set their hands and seals the day and year above written.

| Signed, sealed and delivered by the said | Benjamin Marriner |
| Benjamin Marriner, William Marriner | Wm Marriner |
| And Wm Sinclair | Wm Sinclair |
| In my presence | John Alcock |

Manchester warehouse owners received, was valuable experience because it was the draper's business to find out where the best goods were made. From their knowledge of both materials and the markets they could organise the production of those goods in demand and thus make a profit from handling them.

After finishing his apprenticeship in 1780 William Marriner went to London for reasons which are unclear. During the few months he was there he associated with a man called Jack Proctor. Proctor had the use of Swinsted Hall, which he had borrowed from its owner, Sir James Marriott, who was a judge at the Old Bailey and busy there on Admiralty work. If this is illustrative of the sort of social circles William Marriner was able to move in, it would suggest that he was not without financial resources sufficient to support his later commercial and manufacturing undertakings. There is other evidence that William Marriner had spare capital. About 1800 he lent money to the partnership which ran Westhouse Flax Mill at Blubberhouses. The partners were Thomas Colbeck, Rowland Watson, William Holdsworth, John Holdsworth and Jacob Wilkes. His partner at Grove Mill, David Illingworth, witnessed the agreement.

William Marriner returned to Yorkshire and went into partnership with Ann Illingworth who was probably a widow. They had a shop at Church Green in Keighley where they traded as 'Mercers, Drapers and Grocers'. William Marriner had recently finished his apprenticeship, he appeared to have had some capital, or possibly access to some through his family, so it would seem logical to take up a partnership in an established business following the death of Ann Illingworth's husband. She was the daughter of Joseph Smith who, in 1783, built Castle Mill on North Beck for cotton spinning. Mrs Illingworth had two sons, William and David and when they were old enough they helped with the running of Castle Mill together with William Marriner. That would probably be about 1790. William Marriner was therefore a partner in two enterprises, a draper's shop and a cotton Mill. In 1795 or before it was decided to build a new mill and move from Castle Mill, which was then taken over by Joseph Driver who had previously rented part of it. Ann Illingworth provided the capital for this new mill, which was called Grove Mill, and was built about half a mile upstream from Greengate Mill. This was a four-storey mill measuring fifty-seven feet by thirty-two feet, again was built for cotton spinning, and was occupied by Illingworths & Marriner. After William Marriner's death his two sons joined the partnership. Cotton spinning continued until about 1820 when it was bought by Robert & John Clough and converted to spin worsted.

The two formal partnerships were eventually dissolved on the 27 December 1821 with the following entries in the *London Gazette*.

Notice is hereby given, that the Partnership heretofore carried on by Ann Illingworth and William Marriner, both deceased, as Cotton-Spinners and Cotton-Manufacturers at Groves Mill, near Keighley, in the County of York, under the firm of Illingworth and Marriner, and afterwards by David Illingworth, William Illingworth, deceased, and the said William Marriner, under the firm of

Illingworths and Marriner, and lately by the said David Illingworth, William Illingworth, and also Ann Marriner, Benjamin Flesher Marriner, and William Marriner (the Widow and Sons of the said William Marriner, deceased), under the firm last mentioned, was dissolved on the 27th day of December last past; and that all debts owing by or to the said Partnership will be paid and received by the said David Illingworth: As witness our hands this 2d day of January 1822.

> David Illingworth
> Surviving Executor of Ann Illingworth
> Henry Flesher
> Ann Marriner
> Surviving Executors of William Illingworth
> David Illingworth
> Susannah Illingworth
> Widow and Administratrix of William Illingworth
> Henry Flesher
> Ann Marriner
> Surviving Executors of William Marriner
> David Illingworth
> Susannah Illingworth
> Widow, &c. as above
> Ann Marriner
> Benjn. F. Marriner
> Wm. Marriner, jun.

Notice is hereby given, that the Partnership heretofore carried on by Ann Illingworth and William Marriner, both deceased, as Mercers, Drapers and Grocers, at Keighley, in the County of York, under the firm of Illingworth and Marriner, and afterwards by David Illingworth, William Illingworth, deceased, and the said William Marriner, under the firm of Illingworths and Marriner, was dissolved on the 27th day of December last past; and that all debts owing by or to the said Partnership will be paid and received by the said David Illingworth: As witness our hands this 2d day of January 1822.

> David Illingworth
> Surviving Executor of Ann Illingworth
> Henry Flesher
> Ann Marriner
> Surviving Executors of William Marriner
> David Illingworth
> Susannah Illingworth
> Widow and Administratrix of William Illingworth
> Henry Flesher
> Ann Marriner
> Surviving Executors of William Marriner.

If we return to William Marriner as a young man when he married Ann Flesher in 1792, it can be seen that he already had experience as a cotton spinner and could therefore actively take up his wife's one-third share in Greengate Mill. The firm then became Blakeys & Marriner. William and Ann Marriner lived at Greengate House and had four children. One of them, Sarah, died in 1808, while the other daughter, Margaret, married John Brigg who became one of the leading manufacturers in Keighley. The two boys, Benjamin Flesher and William started working life as worsted manufacturers, but eventually bought the shares of their father's partners and the family gained total control of Greengate Mill in 1817 when the firm became known as B & F Marriner.

**Table 4.1. Partnership changes 1784–1817**

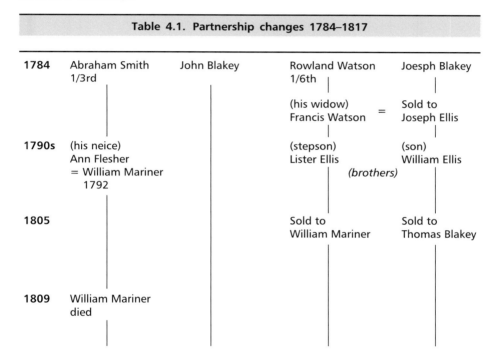

| 1784 | Abraham Smith 1/3rd | John Blakey | Rowland Watson 1/6th | Joesph Blakey |
|------|---------------------|-------------|----------------------|---------------|
|      |                     |             | (his widow) Francis Watson = | Sold to Joseph Ellis |
| 1790s | (his neice) Ann Flesher = William Mariner 1792 | | (stepson) Lister Ellis *(brothers)* | (son) William Ellis |
| 1805 | | | Sold to William Mariner | Sold to Thomas Blakey |
| 1809 | William Mariner died | | | |

John Blakey's one-third share from 1784 remained in his hands until 1817 when it was sold to B & F Marriner. Rowland Watson's one-sixth share passed to his wife on his death and then to her step-son Lister Ellis on her second marriage to Joseph Ellis. Ellis had bought Joseph Blakey's one-sixth share and this in turn went to his other son William. Lister and William Ellis were leading cotton manufacturers in the area with strong associations with the Greenwoods and interests in large cotton mills at Burley-in-Wharfedale and Bingley as well as Keighley. Lister Ellis sold his one-sixth share to William Marriner in 1805 and at the same time his brother sold his one-sixth share to Thomas Blakey. George Beck, Richard Williamson and Jonas Blakey Hardisty who were Thomas Blakey's executors then sold this to B & F Marriner in 1817. When William Marriner bought the one-sixth share from Lister Ellis for £735 he was given £25 back, presumably out of good will. However, the money was not paid at once but in instalments. John Blakey's sale of his share of the mill also had a caveat.[3]

> Mr Blakey engages to relinquish to Mr William & Mr Benjamin Marriner the whole of the mill, stones, wood, machinery, old and new, together with all & everything belonging to the Greengate Concern as it now stands; except one roving frame in the state of preparation it now is for the further sum of twenty pounds in addition to the sum as specified in a former agreement. 7th June 1817 Witness – George Beck

William Marriner died in 1809 when his two sons were fourteen and twelve. According to Hodgson the two boys did not go into cotton but started in business as worsted manufacturers in 1815.

> They bought their first wool in the above year, employing a number of hand combers and hand loom weavers, getting their yarn spun on commission till the year 1818, when they began to spin their own yarn at West Greengate Mill. The class of goods they made from 1815 to 1824, consisted of tammies, dobbies and plainbacks, a class of goods then generally made in this district. From 1824 to 1835, they made tammies, dobbies, plainbacks, shalloons and damasks, when the weaving was given up.[4]

There can be no doubt that there was ample opportunity for the two young men to set up in business as worsted manufacturers in 1815. Their mother had money and presumably could be relied upon for the initial capital with which to buy wool and finance the various processes before the finished cloth was eventually sold. The end of the long war period in 1815 brought about an increase in trade. The industry was well established in the area and had more than doubled in output in the locality in the previous five years. The town was full of people who were well acquainted with the trade and could explain what to do and they already had access to warehouse premises. The thirty-year boom in cotton spinning and weaving in Keighley was coming to an end, as worsted re-established its position as the dominant trade. In addition, Greengate Mill was being run by their father's partners following his death and they may have needed to establish a separate business although they were involved in cotton spinning as partners with the Illingworths at Grove Mill further up the river where they owned a one-third share.

Benjamin and William Marriner's first weavers started in May 1814, not 1815, and the weaver's book shows how the brothers employed between eighty and ninety weavers in the two years between 1814 and 1816. Apart from a few exceptions where weavers lived out of Keighley in places such as Morton, Bingley and Silsden all the others lived in areas of Keighley, some of which are recognisable to-day. Nancy Weaversley was at Church Green, Ellen Wild near the Hope & Anchor and Martha Gill at Guard House. John Sugden was at Coney Lane, Thomas Tindall at Exley Head and Benjamin Smith at Park Lane. Several weavers lived in Wellington Street, Park Lane, Club Houses and Hainsworth Shay. There is the occasional mention of weaving tammies and plainbacks, which substantiates Hodgson's comments. Many of the weavers lived near the mill at Greengate and the book finishes with a short list of 'reeds in weavers' hands'. Overall the book spans the years from 1814 to 1829 but only gives an overall impression of the Marriner's weaving activities. A good number of weavers worked for them. These weavers were locally based and they were weaving the types of cloth, which were in demand at the time.

## The start of worsted spinning and weaving, 1818–36

According to the evidence given to the Factory Commissioners in 1833 Greengate Mill was first used for spinning worsted in 1818. This dating is substantially corroborated by the fact that the first entries in the mill stock book, relatting to the spinning of worsted, occur in December 1818. These entries were for various types of wool and tops, soap for washing the wool, hand combs and a stock of 63 plain backs and 40 wild boars which were types of worsted cloth. Benjamin and William Marriner would have had these already as they had been in business as worsted manufacturers since 1814, but these entries were now in the mill stock book rather than in their own separate accounts.

What happened at Greengate Mill was typical of Keighley's early cotton mills. Originally built during the cotton-spinning boom from 1780 to 1810, they were gradually turned over to worsted spinning or other uses depending on their location and size. The period after about 1815 saw the decline of cotton spinning in Keighley and some other areas of Yorkshire, with businesses incurring heavy losses and many changing hands. The cotton industry, which had spread rapidly throughout the Craven and Yorkshire Dales, into the East and North Ridings and to such places as Conisborough and Doncaster, slowly retreated to the Lancashire boundary areas of Craven and the upper Calder Valley. By 1815 the balance was changing in Keighley, for although both cotton and worsted mills were well established, the domestic worsted industry had grown alongside the new cotton mills and the adaptation of cotton spinning machinery resulted in a drive to build more worsted mills.

Baines Directory of 1822 lists only four cotton-spinning firms in Keighley, but eighteen worsted spinners and manufacturers. As well as the new worsted mills built in the Keighley area up to about 1820, most of the original cotton mills had been changed to worsted, including Greengate Mill. The amount of wool processed in the Yorkshire worsted area increased by 20% between 1810 and 1815 and the Keighley area was responsible for the third largest share of wool used after Bradford and Halifax. Of the total drawback of £6,035 in tax paid in 1815 in respect of the soap used for washing wool, the Bradford area received £1,485, Halifax £1,419 and Keighley £944.

As Keighley lay within both the cotton and worsted areas and as the capital outlay necessary to change from the production of cotton yarn to worsted yarn was not great, the deciding factor was usually the profit available. Several firms produced both cotton and worsted goods, but the general trend at this time in the area was away from cotton towards worsted.

The early value of water power was reduced following the wider use of steam power after 1800 when Boulton & Watt's domination of the steam engine market finished. Spinning mills no longer had to be on streams and rivers, but the investment in dams, water courses and water wheels meant that water power was widely used for many more years. Where steam power was used to supplement the power of a water wheel, transport costs of the coal had to be taken into account when there was no local source. In addition, transport costs for raw materials to more remote locations became an additional burden as production costs were lowered with more efficient machinery. A further factor that brought about the demise of many early mills was that they were built of a size to accommodate simple machinery. As spinning frames were improved, for example, they were made longer with larger numbers of spindles, they would not fit into the early mills. Because of this, one of the interesting facts about the early cotton industry is that the remains of more original mills can be found in Yorkshire than in Lancashire. As can be seen from Table 4.3 water power was to remain important in Keighley for much of the early nineteenth century.

The early resistance to power driven spinning machinery in Lancashire was eventually overcome, although similar resistance to power looms was to surface in the mid-1820s. The machine breaking and rioting of 1779 was forgotten and the widespread use of steam power in larger mills meant that Lancashire became pre-eminent in cotton textiles during the nineteenth century. At the same time new worsted mills were being built in West Yorkshire with the improved version of Arkwright's water-frame, the throstle, being used. By 1820 Bradford had become the centre for the worsted industry in Britain and the manufacturers of Keighley and Haworth began to use Bradford Piece Hall instead of Halifax Piece Hall to sell their cloth. Keighley's early lead over Bradford was lost when steam power became more readily available. None of the textile mills in the town of Bradford was water powered and the steam mills there had the advantage of readily available coal from the pits in such areas as Wibsey and Low Moor. Coal for the Keighley mills was supplied to a certain extent from the small pits at Denholme and Riddlesden, a little way out of the town, but it was more likely to come by canal or cart from Leeds or Bradford. Judging by

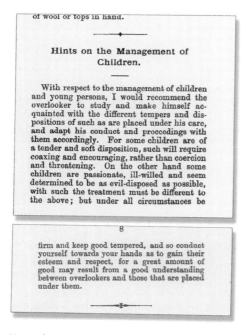

of wool or tops in hand.

**Hints on the Management of Children.**

With respect to the management of children and young persons, I would recommend the overlooker to study and make himself acquainted with the different tempers and dispositions of such as are placed under his care, and adapt his conduct and proceedings with them accordingly. For some children are of a tender and soft disposition, such will require coaxing and encouraging, rather than coercion and threatening. On the other hand some children are passionate, ill-willed and seem determined to be as evil-disposed as possible, with such the treatment must be different to the above; but under all circumstances be

8

firm and keep good tempered, and so conduct yourself towards your hands as to gain their esteem and respect, for a great amount of good may result from a good understanding between overlookers and those that are placed under them.

Notes from 'Bailey's managers' and overlookers' Assistant' owned by H.A. Mariner in 1887 the amount of drawback on the tax for washing wool, the Keighley manufacturers benefited from the rise of Bradford and greatly extended their trade. As can be seen from Table 4.2 the amount of wool processed in the Keighley area doubled between 1810 and 1820 and increased by about 65% in the next ten years.

| Table 4.2. Drawback of tax paid on soap used in the preparation of wool (This indicates the amount of wool used) | | |
|---|---|---|
| Year | Keighley Town | Keighley Area |
| 1810 | £199 | £695 |
| 1815 | £514 | £944 |
| 1820 | £848 | £1,395 |
| 1825 | £1,224 | £1,936 |
| 1830 | £1,866 | £2,391 |

Figures from James, *History of the Worsted Manufacture in England*

This progress was not without the occasional setback for there were several years when demand fell away and manufacturers were left holding large stocks of unwanted wool, yarn and cloth. The worst year was 1826, which followed a year or so of agitation by wool combers and hand loom weavers to obtain an increase in wages. The combers formed an association in August 1824 and then persuaded the hand loom weavers to join them. It was estimated that within a few miles of Bradford over twenty thousand workers were involved.[5] Negotiations between employers and workers failed, and strikes resulted, with the masters in Bradford warning that power loom weaving was starting to reduce costs, although the use of power looms for worsted weaving must have been very limited. Wages were slightly lower in Halifax and Keighley, but spinners and manufacturers in both towns held meetings to canvas support for the Bradford masters by ceasing to employ any workers who assisted the union in any way.

A meeting of the worsted spinners and manufacturers of Keighley and neighbourhood, was convened on the 6th of September (1825) to take into consideration the circular of the Bradford masters, at which a resolution was passed determining to turn off all workpeople who were in the combers' and weavers' Union, and also all those who could be ascertained to support the Union in any manner whatever. This resolution was signed by the following parties:- W. Sugden; J. Greenwood; G. Townend and Brothers; J. Craven; H. Clapham and Sons; J. Mitchell; T. Pearson and Sons; W. Smith and Son; R. Robinson; R. Smith; I. Sharp; J. Illingworth and Co; T. Sugden and Son; W. Haggas; W. and J. Sharp; J. W. Maud; J. Butterfield; R. Clough; W. Lund; P. Hartley and Son; I. Brigg; D. Butterfield; W. Barrett; J. Greenwood; G. Tweedy; Turner and Clough; Nicholls and Maud; T. Jowett; E. Berwick; R. Sharp; J. Townend; W. Robinson; G. Robinson; I. Sutcliffe; Jonas Sutcliffe; W. Heaton; J. Ackroyd; W. Wright; J. Feather; J. Pighills; J. Ogden; R. Ogden; J. Feather; N. Ogden; J. Hanson; J. Clough; J. Anderton; J. Spence;

J. Whitely; T. Ackroyd and Co; A. Tempest; B. Smith; Waley and Ambler; G. Anderton; and J. Barker.[6]

Marriners apparently were not at this meeting and it is interesting to link the names in the list above with the mills which were operating in, and near Keighley, at the time. These would all be spinning mills and are in the Keighley/Haworth area unless stated otherwise. However, some of the men were manufacturers, who bought in yarn or had it spun on commission, kept their stock in a warehouse, and employed hand loom weavers.

| | |
|---|---|
| W Sugden | Fleece Mill |
| J Greenwood | Vale Mill. Cotton spinners and manufacturers |
| G Townend & Brothers, Cullingworth | Heald Yarn Manufacturers |
| J Craven | Walk Mill |
| H Clapham & Sons | Aireworth Mill |
| J Mitchell | Hope Mill |
| T Pearson & Sons | Steeton Mill. Worsted Spinners and Manufacturers |
| W Smith & Son | Leeds Street, Manufacturer |
| R Robinson | Hill Top Mill |
| R Smith | Hoyle House, Exley Head. Manufacturer |
| I Sharp | Possibly J Sharp & Son. Worsted Spinners, Bingley |
| J Illingworth & Co. | Oldroyd Mill, Micklethwaite, Bingley |
| T Sugden & Son | Possibly a manufacturer at Lane Ends |
| W Haggas | Springhead Mill |
| W & J Sharp | Bingley |
| J W Maude | Bingley |
| J Butterfield | Mill on Halifax Road, Keighley |
| R Clough | Grove Mill. Worsted Spinners and Manufacturers |
| W Lund | Holme House Mill |
| P Hartley & Son | Possibly at Sutton |
| I Brigg | Possibly a miss-print for J Brigg at Brow End Mill |
| D Butterfield | Mill on Halifax Road, Keighley |
| W Barrett | Low Street, Keighley |
| J Greenwood | Old Oxenhope Mill |
| G Tweedy | Old Mill, Wilsden |
| Turner & Clough | Possibly at Cross Hills |
| Nicholls & Maude | Possibly at Morton |
| T Jowett | Not traced |
| E Berwick | Cottingley |
| R Sharp | Manufacturer, Park Lane, Keighley |
| J Townend | Possibly at Cullingworth |
| W Robinson | Brandy Mill |
| G Robinson | Not traced |
| I Sutcliff | Possibly at Haworth |
| Jonas Sutcliff | Haworth |
| W Heaton | Possibly Michael Heaton, Royd House Mill |

| J Ackroyd | Far Oxenhope |
|---|---|
| W Wright | Top maker, Silsden |
| J Feather | Hope Mill, Keighley |
| J Pighills | Not traced |
| J Ogden | Manufacturer and spinner, Haworth |
| R Ogden | Manufacturer, Far Oxenhope |
| J Feather | Far Oxenhope |
| N Ogden | Possibly related to the Ogdens above |
| J Hanson | Manufacturer, Nelson Street (Sold yarn to Marriners) |
| J Clough | Grove Mill |
| J Anderton | Cullingworth |
| J Spence | Not traced |
| J Whitley | Micklethwaite, Bingley |
| T Ackroyd & Co. | Possibly at Far Oxenhope |
| A Tempest | Not traced |
| B Smith | Acres Mill |
| Waley & Ambler | Possibly at Harden |
| G Anderton | Piece maker, Keighley |
| J Barker | Not traced |

In the following year, 1826, there was a general depression in trade which had a severe impact on the local textile industry. Probably the most important local feature was the failure of the large firm of Butterworth Brothers who were merchants with premises at Shelf, between Bradford and Halifax, and Lawrence Lane in London. They bought much of the output of local manufacturers, both cotton and worsted, and checking through the pages of Hodgson for details of the manufacturers listed above provides several stories of financial disaster.

Richard Robinson ... was looked up to as a successful man of business till the melancholy panic of 1826, when, having sold most of his pieces to that unfortunate firm, Messrs. Butterworths, their stopping payment gave him a terrible shake.[7]

Richard Robinson was bankrupt in May 1826.[8]

Robert Smith ... passed the panic of 1826 without any serious loss, while numbers of his neighbours were ruined by the failure of the notorious Butterworths; and it is somewhat a remarkable fact that he did not loose a single penny by those unfortunate merchants.[9]

John Hanson ... did not want quite £20 of Messrs. Butterworths when they failed, yet a considerable number of manufacturers who had obtained yarn from him were ruined during the panic, and the very heavy losses entailed upon him by the failure of those piece-makers, so dried up his resources (and especially the heavy loss occasioned by the depreciation of stock) and brought in their train such a financial embarrassment, that, although he tided over the panic, and was able to continue in business a few years longer, yet he was so paralized by the losses sustained during that year, that he never recovered his former standing, and about 1830 was compelled to place his affairs in the hands of his creditors.[10]

John Hanson, a customer of Marriners, was a worsted manufacturer employing large numbers of weavers and also some smaller manufacturers. Unlike Marriners he put out his wool to combers some distance away from Keighley. Hodgson recorded that:

> a number of these combers were what were called 'basketeers', many of them being small farmers living in the country, who used to bring their horse and cart about once a fortnight, with about 200 or 300 pounds weight of tops, which had been combed by them, assisted by their families, returning home again taking back a quantity of wool, with the requisite amount of oil and soap. Some of these 'basketeers' came for their work a considerable distance, even as far as from Nesfield, near Addingham. He also employed about 300 weavers at this time; he had no mill but had his yarn spun by Berry Smith, and Messrs. Marriners, of West Greengate Mill.[11]

John Hanson owed £236 to Marriners in 1822, £279 in 1823, £302 in 1824, £122 in 1825, £29 in 1826, £133 in 1827, £4 in 1828 and nothing thereafter. He was bankrupt in 1830.

The general depression in trade led to a large number of bankruptcies in Keighley and other areas. Unemployment rose and wages fell, particularly for hand loom weavers, who were subject to great competition for work, and also the growing threat of the more widespread use of power looms. An attempt had been made to introduce worsted power looms in Shipley in by James Swarbrick 1822 but they were broken up by hand loom weavers.[12] John Horsfall made his own worsted looms and started using them in Bradford in 1824, but rioters tried to storm the mill in 1826 with two being killed.[13] Cotton power looms were well established, but the distress in 1826 brought rioters from Lancashire to attack mills in Gargrave and Addingham, which had cotton power, looms. At Mason's Mill in Gargrave 300 men broke up twenty looms and other machinery, but they did not succeed in entering Low Mill at Addingham, which was well defended by the militia. Worsted power looms were not used in Keighley until nearly ten years later.

Two further events compounded the effect of the 'Butterworth Panic', as it became known locally. There was a run on the banks with one of the major local banks, Wentworth, Chaloner & Co. ceasing payments and thus taking the resources of all those who had accounts there. Secondly there was a serious drought starting in May which not only stopped canal transport, which was very important at the time, but also stopped many of the water wheels at the mills. A quarter of the workers in Keighley were unemployed by July with only the wealthy Greenwood family not cutting hours or stopping the mill completely. By August the *Leeds Mercury* reported that the 'water mills are rendered totally inactive'.[14] The relative importance of water a decade later can be seen from the next table – Table 4.3

| Year | Mills | Steam engines | Steam h.p. | Water wheels | Water h.p. | Children 9–11 | Persons 11–18 | Total Hands |
|------|-------|--------------|-----------|-------------|-----------|--------------|--------------|-------------|
| 1833 | 22 | 9 | 108 | 15 | 181 | 55 | 613 | 1,061 |
| 1838 | 38 | 16 | 217 | 19 | 207 | 275 | 1,143 | 2,125 |

Table 4.3. Details of Mills in Keighley in 1833 and 1838

The relative position of Keighley in relation to the other West Riding towns was summed up by Hodgson:

> Whilst water continued the principal element of power, Keighley appears to have taken the lead in the spinning department; but, in consequence of Bradford and Halifax being better situated for coal, when the steam engine came into use for mill power, Keighley was left in the rear, still this town maintains its rank as the third manufacturing town in the worsted trade.[15]

Once Benjamin and William Marriner came into complete possession of Greengate Mill in June 1817 they changed most of the rooms over to worsted spinning. There are no stock records for 1817, but at the end of 1818 they still had £348 worth of old machinery and had four new cotton throstles valued at £205. However, there is no mention of these throstles after 1821, or anything else to do with the preparing or spinning of cotton, so it seems that they pursued a rapid run down of cotton spinning and concentrated on worsted yarn.

The cost to Marriners of starting worsted spinning in 1818 is not known. They had to buy half the mill together with the machinery and stock and pay for new machinery. Presumably they already had some stocks of wool and hand combs from their own business. Fortunately for them 1818 was later described as ... the most extraordinary epoch on the earlier history of the worsted manufacture.[16] The reason for that was the great increase in domestic and foreign demand together with a general easing of credit. To cope with the increased demand there had been improvements in the preparing and spinning machinery which were described as ... *a new era*. The decision to change to worsted spinning was taken at the right time.

Greengate Mill was one of the largest mills in the area for the first fifty years of its existence. Even in 1833, when returns were made to the Factory Commissioners, only one other mill, Fleece Mill, which was built in 1820, employed more people and had more power to drive it. Fleece Mill had a 30 h.p. water wheel, the same as Greengate Mill, but it also had a 12 h.p. steam engine. It was another four years before expansion at Greengate brought the need for a 30 h.p. steam engine.

A scrap of paper with some calculations, possibly from 1819, throws some light on how Marriners started. Room and power were let out to three other spinners. This may have been a carry over from previous years and nothing new, but an income from rents enabled the two brothers to start in a small way for the first year or so. Letting out room and power then continued for several more years.

| | | |
|---|---|---|
| William Barrett | 380 spindles | £114.0.0 |
| +Steam apparatus | | |
| John Croft | 440 spindles | £133.4.0 |
| +house and warehouse | | £5.0.0 |
| John Wilkinson | 680 spindles | £102.0.0 |
| +steam apparatus | | |
| B & W M rent | 748 spindles | £224.8.0 |
| +steam apparatus | | |

This practice continued and in 1825 an agreement was made with Thomas Robinson for him to occupy part of the third room at the mill.[17]

A memorandum of an agreement made the 16th day of May 1825 between B & W Marriner on the one part and Thomas Robinson of Keighley on the other part as follows:

> B & W M agree to let JR a part of the 3rd room in Greengate Mill with power to turn 8 worsted spinning frames containing [blank] spindles, and no less quantity, for a period of five years as from the first day of May 1825 at a regular throstle speed 12 hours each day, the regular holidays excepted at the rate of 6/– [30p] per spindle per annum. And in case there should not be sufficient water at particular seasons of the year to run at the regular speed, such deficiency or loss of time to be made up when there is water to spare. It is agreed that JR shall keep all the windows, floors and the interior part of the room in good repair. There are, when entered to, 50 cracked panes of glass in a less or greater degree and that he shall not suffer the children or workpeople to wear any spurred or ironed cloggs during their work.
>
> B & W M agree to clean, oil and keep in repair the tumbling shafts and heavy gearing but not the drawing shafts which are also fixtures.

Thomas Robinson was a commission spinner who later moved to Fleece Mills.

In 1818 the following processes were carried out. Raw wool was stored in the separate warehouse and sorted there. A stock of soap was kept for scouring. Some combing, which was to remain a hand process for many more years, was carried out in the mill or nearby '3 setts combs at £4.10.0' with a 'Combers Ring and Pan £2.0.0' together with £10 worth of charcoal. Two frames were used for drawing while a further seven frames containing 528 spindles were used for spinning. The yarn was then woven into cloth but not, of course, at the mill as weaving was still carried out by the weavers in their own homes. According to the stock record, warps to the value of £46 6s. od. and weft to the value of £23 16s. od. were in the hands of the weavers. On hand were a number of woven pieces – 63 plain backs at £1 12s. od. (£1.60) each and 40 wild bores at £1 10s. 6d. (£1.52)

The mill premises in 1818 had changed little since 1785. There was the main five-storey mill with the water wheel at the southern end and at the northern end a small counting house. The warehouse, at a right angle to the mill, was used for storing wool and also had a comb shop. The top floor of the mill was used for storing the combed tops before they were taken to the floors below for preparing and spinning. On the ground floor was a taking-in room and below that a room for washing and sizing. Finally there was a workshop and smithy which was of great importance for many years as the firm continued to make and repair a good deal of its own machinery. For instance in 1832 they had some spinning frames which had been made in their own workshop as well as some modified from twisting frames.

The water wheel was the only source of power for the first fifty years of the mill's existence. Even after the installation of a steam engine in 1837 the water wheel provided power for the old mill and sometimes the new one. It was not taken out until the First World War. However, the wheel needed repairing from time to time and also had to be replaced when repairs were no longer effective. In 1821 a Mr Hardwick wrote from Stamford Bridge with details of a large oak tree which would be suitable for a new axle. Hardwick advised that the tree should be left round to cast the water and said that it could be 2ft 8ins in diameter. There is no record indicating whether or not the Stamford Bridge oak was chosen, but the stock record for December 1821 includes the item 'Wheelaxle and old boards' so a replacement was made.

At about the same time as the water wheel was being repaired or replaced additions were made to the warehouse. These were to increase the space for hand combers by increasing the number of comb shops and the number of hand combs provided for them. The warehouse was extended further in 1831. It does not seem that Greengate Mill had its own generating plant when gas became available in other mills by the late 1820s and early 1830s.[18] However, gas was being bought in 1828 from the Keighley Gas Light Company. Marriners had fifty burners, William Barrett had seven and Thomas Robinson had 14 with a further six in Marriner's comb shop.[19]

From the available details of stock and machinery it would seem that after the start of worsted spinning in 1818 there followed a long period of expansion. The first main process, that of combing, shows this increase. From three pairs of combs in 1818 the number rose to a peak of 70 pairs in 1836–7. Although this indicates an increase in the amount of wool processed it was always possible to give out wool to be combed by self employed-combers in the town. This may have been done, as the number of combs in stock could not have been enough to supply the needs of the spinning section of the firm. However, the number of combs owned by the firm increased far more rapidly than their spinning capacity so it would seem that the tendency was to increase the amount of wool combed at the mill in their own comb shops.

Three sets of combs were worth £4 10s. (£4.50) a pair in 1818 and these, together with a comber's ring at £2 and £10 worth of charcoal, made up the combing side of the business. 20 pairs of 3 pitch combs and 18 pairs of 4 pitch were entered in 1824 but the value of these was only £1 10s. (£1.50) and £1 15s. (£1.75). In the following year 4 pairs of fine 3 pitch combs were added and these in turn were gradually depreciated in the stock-record. In 1829 and 1830 there was an entry for 'Comb pots and posts in Myers house £2'. This probably indicates pressure on the space available as the firm expanded. In 1834 the comb shops were described as being at 'Greengate', in other words away from the mill. This was for insurance purposes as hand combing provided a constant fire risk. By this time the 3 pitch combs were valued at 14s. 0d. (70p) per pair and the 4 pitch at 19s. 0d. (95p). However, the 4 pitch combs were still kept at the mill where the combers had a wash house with scouring rings and bowls for washing the wool. One interesting entry, in a letter giving details of changes for insurance purposes in 1831, explains that they had added another combing machine, which was heated by steam and similar to the one they already had. These combing machines were in a room in the old mill. As hand combing continued for many more years it must be assumed that these early combing machines were not very efficient. The hand combs were usually heated in pots containing charcoal and there is mention of these together with a stock of charcoal. In 1835, besides 2 comb pots for charcoal, there were 2 pots for coal.

In 1827 two carding engines with 'box and clothing' had been added to replace the hand carding process. These were valued at £220 at the end of the year, but this may not have been the cost to them, as it seems that they were made at the mill. One of their mechanics had built the carding machines using castings from Franklands of Coney Lane, a firm of iron founders in Keighley.

These cards were gradually depreciated in the yearly stock records to £120 in 1831. However, in that year another carding machine valued at £150 was added and, in the following year, the card clothing was replaced on the original machines so their value increased. These machines then ran until a new card was added with the general expansion in productive capacity in 1837. The machines may have been of an advanced design for in 1838 Marriners wanted to oppose an application by John & William Butterfield of Prospect Mill, Halifax Road, for a patent for an improved carding machine. This patent was ... For carding wool for the worsted and woollen manufacture by the operation of certain machinery for the clearing of the cylinders so that double the quantity of work may be done in the usual time now exercised without overcharging the cylinder and only the same number of hands required, with very little addition of power.

Marriners were advised to send a sketch and details of their carding engine as soon as possible by a London agent, Mr F Blake of Bedford Row, presumably as proof that they were already using a similar machine.[20]

Although Marriners were worsted cloth manufacturers at this time, the processes carried on in the mill were all related to spinning and there was a six-fold increase in spindle capacity between 1818 and 1837. Marriners started worsted spinning in 1818 with seven frames containing a total of 528 spindles. These frames were valued at £1 per spindle and from their valuation it is possible to trace them through to 1836. The original seven frames were added to by others of a similar type, which were classified with them for stocktaking purposes. Thus the original seven frames were added to in 1819, 1820, 1821 and 1823 by which time there were fourteen. Another was added in 1831, but by then they were worth only 13s. 0d. (65p) per spindle. These frames continued in use until at least 1838, by which time many new and second-hand frames had been bought to supplement the original equipment. Other frames were added as production expanded but these were usually classified separately, sometimes with a note about their origin.

From only one type of spinning frame in 1818 a series of additions, particularly in the 1830s, resulted in fifteen different types of spinning and twisting frames being used by 1836. The sources of these frames illustrate how the firm often bought second-hand machines or made their own, despite the growth of machine making firms in Keighley. For instance, in 1829 a 96-spindle frame was bought from a mill in Morton, an industrial village a few miles away. This was valued at only 5s. (25p) per spindle but in the following year new top rollers were added and it then continued in use until 1838. Similarly in 1831 a frame with 60 spindles was bought from Lumbfoot Mill further up the valley. This was valued at 3s. 6d. (17p) a spindle in 1831 and carried on until 1836, by then valued at only 1s. (5p) per spindle. The firm's workshop gained an increasing amount of machine tools to construct and maintain the preparing and spinning frames. This included 'laithes', 'turning tools', 'gantry' and a large stock of brass, iron, wood together with rollers and flyers. To help with the construction of new machines the workshop also had 'Moddles' valued at £5 in 1835. As it was possible to construct their own machinery, buy second-hand or update existing machines, little was bought new. Exceptions were in 1827 when three new frames were bought and probably in 1835 when a frame was described as 'new from Bradford'.

The growth in the number and type of spinning frames was necessary as the firm started to produce a greater variety of yarns. Initially the major part of their production was yarn for weaving into cloth by hand loom weavers. In 1825 they started making heald yarn which was used in a device called a heald which raises and lowers the warp threads in a loom. At the same time they started producing genapped yarns, which were used for making fringes, braids, carpets and hosiery. The genappe process involved using heat to remove slight imperfections from the yarn to give a smooth finish. 1833 saw the addition of soft yarns used for hand knitting and crochet work.

The years from 1832 to 1836 were described as *'among the most prosperous period in the history of the West Riding stuff trade.'* The high level of demand from both the home and foreign markets encouraged spinners and manufacturers to expand their mills and also encouraged new firms to enter the trade. Marriners, however, decided to run down their weaving activities. This was done very rapidly between 1834 and 1835 at a time when power looms were being introduced into other mills in Keighley. This was a major decision, which meant that they could not benefit directly from the increased demand for worsted cloth. However, the demand for heald yarn from the heald manufacturers and the users of looms increased, as did the demand for warp and weft to be used by local manufacturers, some of which was spun on a commission basis. Marriners had also established themselves in the growing market for soft yarns for hand working which became very popular with Victorian ladies. All these factors must have influenced their decision to abandon weaving and expand the mill premises to produce more of their growing range of yarns.

The stock books show a considerable increase in the amount of machinery used in the original mill after 1818. An extension was built at the south end of the mill in 1821 and let out to John Croft until 1826. He had been in a partnership, which traded as Messrs Croft & Clough, but they were bankrupt in 1826. Their worsted machinery was for sale and included some frames made by Mr F Sleddon.[21] Marriners took the room for themselves and may have bought the machinery. The number of spindles increased steadily and was accompanied by a comparable addition in preparing. As an example of this, the 'Fourth Room' in the mill, which held eleven spinning frames in 1820 contained these eleven and four others in 1835, together with drawing, slubbing and roving frames. The water wheel was replaced again in 1834, possibly with one of greater power, but it was soon to be supplemented with the addition of a steam engine. A point had been reached where a new mill had to be built and that needed more power.

## The first steam engine

When Marriners decided to buy a steam engine for their new mill they went about it in characteristic style. Quotations were obtained in 1836 from seven firms in different parts of the country for a 30 h.p. engine, together with the necessary boilers. The letters from the various firms gave details of their engines, boilers and transport costs. Some gave details of the size of cylinder, air pump, condenser and flywheel while others concentrated on the terms of payment.

Quotations were supplied by:[22]

| Firm | Place | Price quoted |
|------|-------|-------------|
| Peel, Williamson & Co. | Manchester | |
| Lawson & Co. | Leeds | |
| Bowling Iron Works | Bradford | |
| William Fairburn | Manchester | £1,220 |
| B Hick & Co. | Bolton | £1,230 |
| Galloway, Bowman & Glasgow | Manchester | £1,100 |
| Haigh Foundry | Wigan | £970 |

In addition quotations were obtained from Haigh Foundry for a 20 h.p. and a 60 h.p. engine before a decision was made to take the 30 h.p. engine. There was little to choose between the various prices quoted, for although the Haigh Foundry price was lower than the others, it excluded the cost of boilers. Marriners favoured the Wigan firm because of letters they received from William Corlass of Preston. A friend of Corlass, Francis Sleddon Jnr, conducted some of the initial enquiries with Haigh Foundry for Marriners. Corlass wrote to say that Mr Sleddon and his son, who he said were well acquainted with steam engines, thought that the prices quoted were reasonable. He added that they ... were of the same opinion with myself that they should have 2 boilers of 20 horse power each and have the boiler house built to hold 3 boilers and you might put the third in at some future period.

Following these good reports Marriners approached Haigh Foundry who agreed to supply a 30 h.p. engine, without boilers for £970. They added that their Mr Fletcher would meet the Marriners when required and would bring the plan of the engine house that had been asked for. The custom of passing on information for friends seems to have common for Haigh Foundry sent an estimate for a 60 h.p. engine which Marriners had requested for an acquaintance.

In November 1836 the agreement was signed with Haigh Foundry for the new engine. This was to be ready by April 1837 provided that the masonry and joiner's work, which had to be arranged by Marriners, was completed on time. Marriners also had to provide labouring assistance and any additional materials required for the erection of the engine. The cost of the engine was to be paid in cash, half when the foundry had completed their part of the work and the other half three months later. A letter from Haigh Foundry gave their requirements:

> The engine would be complete to the end of the fly wheel shaft, would be put on board a boat at Wigan, the expense of carriage to be paid by the purchaser, as well, the stone, brick and carpentry work, labouring assistance etc required for the erection of the engine and have it ready for work in six months from the receipt of the order if not hindered by anything at Keighley.

Drawings were sent from Wigan to Keighley, but these do not survive although there are some pages of comments on them for the use of Marriner's contractor, Edward Craven, when he was supervising the building of the engine house. Besides the detail of the engine and engine house, Craven was also possibly supervising the building of the new mill into which the engine house was integrated. The boilers and chimney were separate with two boilers being used. One was supplied by the Bowling Company of Bradford, to be delivered during March 1837 and was to be 19 feet by 9 feet at a cost of £1 9s. per hundredweight. Haigh Foundry also sent plans of chimneys, which they thought, would be suitable for the site. Their comments included such phrases as ... more handsome looking and the best chimney that could be designed for the situation. Obviously cost and efficiency were not the only considerations although the chimney they were describing was also the cheaper of the two mentioned. The other was dismissed as being ... too low for looking well. Marriners were sent plans of the chimney and of the metal cornice plates, which they were to have cast locally.

Hiram Craven was a well-known local civil engineer and contractor who, together with his sons, built mills, bridges, docks and later, railways.[23] In the Keighley area he built Ebor Mill in 1819, then bought Mytholmes Mill which he enlarged and then rebuilt Higher Providence Mill about 1825.[24] Craven was often consulted by the Greenwoods on water power. He rebuilt Higher Providence Mill with two water wheels, one above the other which was not an unusual arrangement. He was not himself a worsted spinner, but built and owned a number of mills around Keighley.

Estimates for walling and the ashlar bed for the engine were needed and

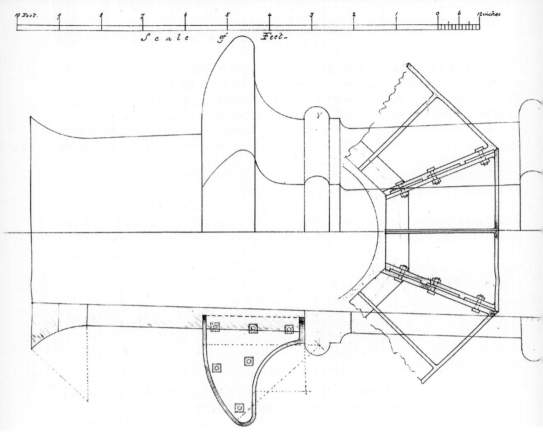

Haigh Foundry's drawing of cornice plates for the new chimney. The plates were to be cast in Keighley.

## Haigh Foundry

Wigan
24th January 1837

B & W Mariner
You have drawing of the chimney top both in section and half round together with a view of the cornice plates showing how they are bolted together which we trust will enable you to get the castings done.

   We are much obliged by the intrest you use in recommending our engines and should be very proud to make one for your – wages and coals are too much advanced that we cannot make engines as low as the price of metal will permit – our price for a 24 horse is £900 Nine Hundred Pounds – with boiler of the same power – or with 2 boilers of 20 Horse Power each it will be £1100 Eleven Hundred ten pounds – If these prices are likely to suit shall be happy to furnish your friend with particulars.

With many thanks we remain yours very respectfully
Haigh Foundry Co.

during December several masons in the Keighley area laboriously put pen to paper and scratched out their quotations for building walls and *'chimleys'*. William Lister Marriner noted in his diary that work stated on the foundations for the engine house on 9 March 1837 and from that point documentary evidence ceases.[25] Clearly the next few months were busy ones at Greengate Mill. The engine parts from Wigan and the boiler from Bradford would have to be brought from the canal at Stockbridge. Gangs of workers would be erecting the new spinning mill while others would be building the chimney and Haigh Foundry's engineers would be putting their engine together. A trench in the mill yard had to be dug so that shafting could be put in to connect the motive power of the old and new mills and all the time production had to be maintained.

After the completion of the new mill the yard had buildings on three sides and the goit on the fourth. The three-storey mill was built in the simple style of most Keighley mills at that period but with the embellishment of an outside staircase surmounted by a bell and clock tower. Within a short time of completion the mill was being used, though the ... new clock complete £10 and ... Bell and Ropes £7 5s. 0d. were not added until 1838.

## Wool purchases

In some ways the methods of purchasing wool became similar to the earlier methods of purchasing cotton with the difference being that the merchants were in Bradford, Halifax or Wakefield rather than Manchester or Liverpool. For instance, by 1836 Marriners had wool in their warehouse at Greengate from Hustler & Blackburn of Bradford, Thomas Milnthorpe & Co. of Bradford,

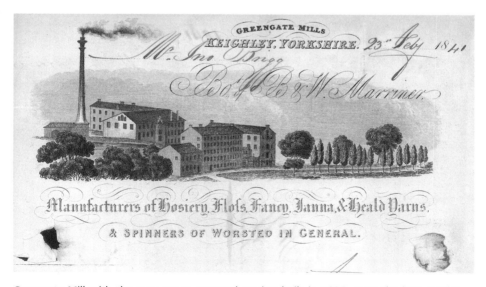

Greengate Mill with the new steam powered section built in 1836. Note the iron cornice on the chimney which corresponds with the drawing opposite.

Benjamin Stocks & Son of Leeds, John Wade of Leeds and J & S Flatman of Wakefield.

However, in the eighteenth century and early part of the nineteenth century there were a number of wool merchants or wool-staplers in Keighley. Hodgson mentions several of these including David Spencer who was the father of Benjamin Marriner's wife. Others were John and Isaac Butterfield, William Sharp, John Sugden and William Roper. William Roper and another wool-stapler, Holmes Clapham bought wool in Lincolnshire, Leicester shire and the East Riding of Yorkshire. They had it brought up the rivers to Leeds, and forwarded by the Leeds and Liverpool Canal to Stock Bridge. The scale of this activity was such that Mr Holmes:

Clock tower at the new mill. The bell hung between the two stones at the top.

... sometimes bought as much as 40 packs at a time, which would be considered a large quantity at that time, when the yarn had all to be spun on the hand wheel one thread at a time. He also sold to Cunliffe & Lister, of Addingham Low Mill, who were the first in Yorkshire to spin worsted by machinery.[26]

This early practice of buying wool in Lincolnshire and East Yorkshire was followed by manufacturers such as James Haggas, John Mitchell and Joshua Cowling, and also by Benjamin and William Marriner. Some of the wool buying trips are well documented with letters between Benjamin as buyer and William who stayed behind to manage the mill. From the letters it can be seen that a number of problems existed. Benjamin had to bargain with the farmers without being sure of the exact quality of all the wool for which he was bidding. He had to use his judgement based on the samples he saw. It was only after the packs of wool had been opened at the mill that its real quality could be ascertained. Then William would write with comments on the wool and give further suggestions as to what to buy and at what price. William was not always impressed with the quality of the wool he received.

Another difficulty arose from the fact that the farmers preferred to be paid in cash, as they were suspicious of the normal trade bills from people they did not know. Even then they wanted notes from a Scarborough bank rather than Marriner's Skipton bank, Chippendale, Netherwood & Carr. This hindrance to trade because of inadequate banking facilities could only be overcome in some villages by the use of letters of introduction. Apparently in one area a letter of introduction from Richard Fawcett, who built the first worsted and cotton spinning mill in Bradford in 1801, would have helped matters, as he had a high reputation among the farmers. Because of the money problems Benjamin's letters to his brother are full of requests for cash so that he could then obtain a lower price.

The wool was packed in hemp sheets for transport, with the buyer providing these, and during the wool buying season there was a shortage. Where possible they were sent on from Keighley, but Benjamin also tried to buy them locally.

Once the wool had been packed, it was sent off by river and canal. Benjamin mentions wool being sent to York and to the canal at Malton. An idea of the time taken for the journey can be gained from the letters written by Benjamin when he combined a wool buying trip with his honeymoon. Benjamin wrote from Scarborough on Saturday 24 June 1822 mentioning that he had been bargaining with Thomas Butterfield for some wool at the village of Huggate which is about midway between York and Bridlington. At the end of his letter he asked for some sheets to be sent to Huggate, presumably for packing the wool he had just bought or to replace the sheets he had used. On 3 July William wrote that they had received the wool on the Monday so it had taken a week to travel to Keighley. It had been brought from Leeds by Sugden Pearson, who was a carrier in Keighley.

Visits to the wool producing areas continued for several years, but the occasional references do not indicate the scale of purchases. Perhaps it was not possible to buy the quantity or quality required from the farmers, although the price was probably lower than had to be paid to the merchants. The more likely explanation is that at shearing time cheaper wool could be bought from the farmers and Marriners took advantage of that and, at the same time, had a break at Scarborough. Despite the price advantage, Marriners probably had neither the capital nor the warehouse capacity to buy enough wool for the whole year so at other times they bought from the wool merchants who carried the commercial risk and could offer a range of qualities. In 1823 Benjamin Marriner wrote to an unknown friend ... It has become customary of late for the farmers to send their wool to Bradford to sell by commisssion.

Although wool buying trips were made for several years, the merchants probably supplied the bulk of the wool bought by Marriners as production expanded. For some years between 1818 and 1832 accounts have survived of the year end balance owed by, and to, B & W Marriner. These sheets of paper can only give an incomplete picture of Marriner's dealings for if there were no outstanding debts at the end of the year there was no sum to record. Large amounts of purchases and sales could therefore be missed, but nevertheless some light is thrown on the trading activities of the firm. One thing that comes out clearly is that from the start they were buying from the Bradford merchants. By December 1827 Marriners owed £1,715 to Hustler & Blackburn of Bradford. This was by far the largest debt outstanding at the end of the year and must represent large purchases during the previous year. A sum of £128 was also owing to Isaac Butterfield who was a wool-stapler in Chapel Lane, Keighley. Ten years later in 1837 wool was still being bought from Hustler & Blackburn, but other merchants also supplied Marriners. Amongst them were William Marten and James Townend of Bradford and B Goodman & Son of Leeds. From the evidence of the year-end accounts it would seem that the tendency was to buy from a greater number of suppliers as the firm expanded.

## Spinning

Apart from the production of warp and weft yarns for their own manufacture of cloth, yarn was also spun for sale and on commission. Cotton spinning continued until 1821 when it was replaced with the production of hosiery yarn. At the end of 1822 there was a stock of worsted hosiery yarn waiting for sale at York. This was followed in 1825 by the spinning of heald and genappe yarn. The equipment to produce these yarns was installed in a new yarn dressing room and at the end of that year heald yarn was being sold in Manchester and Huddersfield. A further development extended the range of speciality yarns for ... In 1826 they commenced making a variety of carded yarns which were sent to London and Manchester, and shortly after to Kidderminster, Leicester and the north.[27]

The production of heald yarn appears to have been on a small scale until 1830 when a determined effort was made to sell this type of yarn. A separate account of customers was begun and continued for some years. The first sales in Manchester and London were followed in 1830 with direct sales to the main users of the yarn. These were the heald makers who supplied both the firms that made looms and any manufacturer who needed a replacement heald. The heald raised or lowered the warp threads each time the shuttle passed from side to side and looms could have several depending on the complexity of the pattern being woven. The yarn was fastened between the top and bottom heald shafts and each length of yarn was given an eyelet or 'mail' for the warp threads to pass through.

The first lists of Marriner's customers for heald yarn, which again are incomplete, were almost exclusively made up of heald makers. The odd one out in 1830 was James Ackroyd of Halifax who was a stuff manufacturer. These first 21 customers were in different parts of the West Riding outside Keighley. Several were near Leeds, John Wood and James Fawcet both of High Wortley, Fawcett was a gear and slay maker, John Hill and Henry Ledger, both gear and slay makers of Bramley, and James Oates, another gear and slay maker of Armley. William Wood and John Ramsden had the same trade in Bradford as did Benjamin Yeadon at Idle on the outskirts. Alfred Clough was a reed maker in Halifax while others were at Gildersome, Golcar and Huddersfield.

The lists of customers for 1831 and 1832 are missing, but one for 1833 shows a considerable expansion in the number of customers and their geographical distribution. The heald and slay makers of the West Riding textile area are well represented but textile firms in other areas were now buying Marriner's heald yarn. These included Walton, Oates & Co. at Castle Mill in Knaresborough who were flax spinners, and James Potts, also of Knaresborough, who was a reed and gear maker, possibly for the numerous linen weavers in the town. The largest number of new customers however, was in Lancashire and Cheshire, including ten cotton spinners and manufacturers in Stockport and Hyde alone. The following year another 35 customers were added, this time mainly in the Lancashire cotton towns of Burnley, Preston, Oldham, Blackburn, Bolton and Colne. The increasing numbers of power looms being produced and used can explain the growth of sales in the cotton textile areas. That was particularly true in the years 1832–34 when many spinning firms added power loom weaving sheds to their existing spinning mills. Many of Marriner's customers were described as cotton spinners in contemporary directories but their purchases of heald yarn indicates that they were in the process of buying looms and adding weaving to their range of activities.

| Table 4.4. Heald yarn sales | |
|---|---|
| Year | Value |
| 1834 | £1,212 |
| 1835 | £1,277 |
| 1836 | £2,220 |
| 1837 | £3,176 |
| 1838 | — |
| 1839 | — |
| 1840 | £2,534 |
| 1841 | £1,841 |

From Table 4.4 it can be seen how sales expanded during the 1830s when power-loom weaving was becoming more widespread. The year 1837 produced total sales of £3,176 to 108 customers. Of these 63 were in the Lancashire-Cheshire cotton towns and a further seven were linen manufacturers in Barnsley which was one of the centres for linen weaving in Yorkshire. Six firms took over £100 worth of yarn. These were:

| | |
|---|---|
| Moorhouse & Pollett, Stockport | £338 |
| John Leach, Stalybridge | £212 |
| James Oates, Armley, Gear and slay maker | £202 |
| James Hyde, Duckinfield, Cotton spinner and manufacturer | £144 |
| John Ramsden, Snr, Bradford, Reed and heald manufacturer | £120 |
| Brown & Powell, Stockport | £105 |

The two textile-engineering firms had been customers for at least seven years, but the other four were more recent examples of the demand from the cotton manufacturers.

The sale of this type of yarn may have been organised through agents. In a letter William Marriner wrote to his brother in 1828, he suggested that Benjamin should call in Preston to see James Dilworth, who was a general agent, to ask if he wanted to be an agent for heald yarn. From 1833 there is a mention of William Nixon receiving 7½% commission on some of the sales so presumably an agent was appointed.

The yarns described so far were generally known as 'hard yarns' as they were smooth, well twisted yarns, which were singed to remove stray fibres. Later a different, softer, type of yarn was spun. Hodgson wrote that ... In 1833 they commenced making soft yarns, commonly called Berlin wool; these fine and soft yarns are extensively used for ladies' knitting and crotchet work, made into a variety of articles too numerous to mention.[28]

Berlin wool was used for embroidery on various backings, using prepared designs on squared paper. Early in the century a Berlin print seller published his first designs, and some were imported, together with the necessary wools. The first Berlin patterns to become readily available were sold in London in 1831 and were very expensive. Very soon the price came down and needlework became a popular activity for the growing number of middle class women in the towns who could afford to employ servants and had plenty of leisure time. By the late 1840s thousands of different patterns had been produced, which were copied in thread after counting the squares on meshed canvas. It was therefore possible to produce a decorative article without having to design it first. By the 1870s colour was used in the patterns and the choice of wool shades was only limited by the number available. Many women gathered together to sew and share their wools. The subjects of the designs were such things as romantic paintings, family pets, the Royal Family and exotic birds. The finished work could be hung on a wall, used as a cushion, for a footstool or as a firescreen. Later designs involved shearing the threads, as with plush, to give a raised effect and this became a characteristic of Berlin work. Marriners produced the required soft yarns for Berlin

Berlin wool pattern.

work, which were dyed in strong colours, and they also produced another type called floss yarn.

Marriners sold their soft yarns in Manchester through an agent called James Brown. At the end of 1833 he held £2,523 worth of stock and was still their agent in 1837. Manchester continued to be an important outlet for Marriner's yarns and they eventually established a business address there.

## Weaving

The Marriner brothers were worsted cloth manufacturers from 1814 before they took over complete control of Greengate Mill and continued manu-facturing until it was allowed to run down in 1835. Hodgson listed the kinds of cloth produced by Marriners in those years as … from 1815 to 1824 consisting of tammies, dobbies and plainbacks, a class of goods then generally made in this district. From 1824 to 1835 they made tammies, dobbies, plainbacks, shalloons and damasks, when the weaving was given up.[29]

The stock record confirms this but with the addition of a large number of pieces called wildbores, some merinos and an occasional serge. Further confirmation comes from lists of equipment, which show that in 1819 they had loom gears for making drawboys, dobbies, plain backs and wildbores.

The organisation of this activity involved the use of a taking-in room at the mill. The weavers attended there to pick up their warp and weft and return the pieces of cloth they had woven. They were paid for each piece and worked independently of the mill, usually in their own homes. Many of them owned their own looms, but some used looms which belonged to Marriners. If the weavers were self-employed they could please themselves whose yarn they wove. Thus some weavers' names appeared only once on Marriner's list, but others remained year after year. During the first period from 1814, between eighty and ninety weavers were employed over a two-year period. They lived mainly in the Keighley area with addresses that are recognisable today – Nancy Weaversley, Church Green; Grace Ramsden, Guard House; John Gawthrope, Low Street. Others however, lived further away, e.g. John Lund at Utley; Sarah Taylor at Morton Banks; William Whitley at Bingley.

From 1816 to May 1818 there is a gap in the records, which coincides with Marriner's acquisition of full control of the mill. When the records in the weavers' book recommenced in 1818 the great majority of weavers were new to Marriners. An exception was Susy Butterfield of Malt Kiln who had been paid an average of 2s. 0d. (10p) per piece from 1814 to 1816, but who was being paid from 5s. 0d. (25p) to 6s. 6d. (32p) in 1818 and 1819. Unfortunately it is impossible to establish from any of this evidence the type and quality of the cloth being woven for Marriners. It is interesting to note, however, that about one third of the people who were weaving for Marriners were women. This is not too surprising for women customarily wove some types of cloth at that time, particularly the wildbore, which figured largely in Marriner's stock.

The prices paid for weaving depended on the type of cloth and the quality of the weaving. The accounts merely state a figure with no reference to allowances or deductions. If we accept that the weavers produced fairly standard pieces of cloth the accounts show how the price paid to the weavers rose and fell over the years. For instance, William Arnold of Wellington Street was receiving 5s. 0d. (25p) per piece in August 1819, but the account was then balanced and in December he was paid 8s. 6d. (42p). This amount fell gradually to 6s. 9d. (33p) in December 1821 but in the next month he was being paid 9s. 0d. (45p) and this rose to 11s. 0d. (55p) in March. After a year's gap he was down to 4s. 6d. (22p) in March 1823. The price varied a little through the next year falling eventually to 3s. 6d. (17p) in March 1825. As the price per piece fell, the number of pieces woven per month rose. He wove eight or ten pieces a month at 8s. 0d. (40p) in 1820, fourteen a month in April 1823 at 5s. 0d. (25p) and fifteen a month in March 1825 at 3s. 6d. (17p). In the face of falling prices for weaving he had to work so much harder to make a living unless he had changed to more easily woven pieces. This example was a reflection of the overall situation for the hand loom weavers at the time which led to a great deal of unrest.

One event that has been referred to earlier, the 'Butterworth Panic' of 1826, shows up in weaving prices. Many Keighley manufacturers sold their pieces through these merchants and unfortunately for them, Butterworths went bankrupt. This had a great effect on the town, for Hodgson, writing about Andrew Pearson of Braithwaite, said that ... Like great numbers of his fellow manufacturers during the year 1826 (when it was believed that more than one half of the manufacturers in the town and parish were ruined) he was brought to grief.[30]

This 'panic' shows up in the sums paid to Jane Keighley of Hainsworth Shay who was paid at least 4s. 0d. (20p) per piece by Marriners from 1821 through to 1829 except in 1826, when the price fell to 3s. 6d. (17p) in April, 3s. 3d. (16p) in May, and 3s. 0d. (15p) in June. However, the price rose to over 4s. 0d. (20p) in September when prices returned to normal. Similarly, George Beanlands of Wellington Street, who had received from between 6s. 0d. (30p) and 7s. 0d. (35p) per piece from 1822 to early 1824 found that the price was falling at the end of 1825 and in March 1826 received only 3s. 7½d. (18p). Although prices recovered some months after the bankruptcy of Messrs Butterworth, the general trend during the 1820s was for weaving prices to fall.

The number of weavers employed by Marriners at any one time is difficult to assess. Each entry in the year-end account sheet was given a ledger reference number, but unfortunately none of the ledgers and only one of the account sheets has survived. During the 1820s the number rose to well over 200 but the number actually weaving for Marriners at any one time would be less than that. In December 1823, for example, only 50 weavers had yarn out or owed money to Marriners. This would point to a medium-sized manufacturing enterprise. By comparison, Robert Smith of Keighley, who was also a manufacturer during the early 1820s, was ... considered a large manufacturer at that time, giving employment to no fewer than 200 weavers. It should be remembered though, that Marriners were also commission spinners, with a good part of their yarn being woven up by additional weavers in the employ of other manufacturers, such as John Hanson, who did not run a spinning mill.

Besides paying weavers who owned their own looms, Marriners kept a stock of looms and accessories which they hired out. For instance, at the end of 1819 they had sets of 'Draw Boy' and 'Dobby' gears and, in the following year, healds and slays. In 1824 they had 'New Looms and gears in garret'. The usual parts they kept were healds and slays, and these were part of their stock in the taking-in room until 1835. About that time weaving was given up and the healds and slays were described as 'old'. Some weavers must have travelled some distance to Greengate for in 1828 the stock book mentions healds and slays at Colne and Silsden.

Generally the worsted pieces were sold unfinished, but from 1821 onwards some were dyed. This process was not carried out at the mill but by specialist dying firms. In 1821 there is mention of warp and weft in dyer's hands but piece dying does not seem to have started until 1828. Certain pieces were then described as being 'colours or more specifically as black, brown or crimson.

During the 1820s and 1830s the demand for worsted cloth increased with the growth of markets at home and abroad. The two main Piece Halls for the sale of worsted cloth in the West Riding were at Bradford and Halifax. By 1822, however, Bradford had become the main centre; only 68 manufacturers attended at Halifax whereas 310 attended at Bradford Piece Hall. Of the 310, 33 were Keighley manufacturers including B & W Marriner who could also be contacted at the Bull's Head. Many of the merchants who attended at Bradford's Piece Hall came from Leeds, including Richard Gallon of Park Lane in Leeds. He wrote to Marriners on 12 October 1820 asking them to send whatever pieces they had and to ask Craven & Brigg of Walk Mill, the next mill down the valley, to send whatever they had. In a further letter dated 8 December 1821 he asked for pieces to be sent on as promised and added that he had a 'most particular man waiting'.

It is probable that Marriners sold most of their output of worsted cloth through the Bradford market, but there is no way of substantiating that. The only other place mentioned for selling cloth was Manchester, for there are accounts of stock there from 1829 to 1831. The number of pieces sold there, mainly shalloons, does not seem to have been great.

The figures for worsted pieces in stock at the end of each year from 1818 to 1835, indicate that trade generally increased from 1818 until 1825. That was the year of the great wool combers' strike, which lasted for over four months and consequently caused great disruption to the worsted trade. The following year was the year of the 'Butterworth Panic' mentioned earlier and the reduced stocks probably indicate a general reduction in trade. Two years when stocks of pieces held by the firm were very high were 1828 and 1832. On the one hand it may have been due to a sudden fall in demand leaving Marriners with large stocks or they may have been anticipating demand and built up stocks accordingly. The markets for worsted cloth at this time, both home and foreign, were very volatile with problems in Europe and political unrest in Britain. Labour disputes with another combers' strike in 1832 and falling wages for weavers added to the problems. What is clear is that Marriner's stocks of cloth declined rapidly from 678 pieces in 1834 to 76 in 1835, the last full year that Marriners engaged in weaving.

Weaving was given up in 1836 when the Marriner brothers concentrated on the production of a range of yarns with none being used for the manufacture of their own cloth. The main reason for stopping weaving probably lies in the widespread breakthrough in technology as weaving by hand gave way to weaving by power. Other, neighbouring firms in Keighley, were installing power looms at this time, for example, William Lund at North Beck Mill in 1833, J & J Craven at Walk Mill in 1834 and Robert Clough at Grove Mill in 1836. A new worsted mill built at Sugden's Place in 1834 was advertised as being suitable for worsted spinning and power loom weaving.[31]

To start power loom weaving would have meant an investment in new technology although the new looms were not expensive. For instance Robert Clough at Groves Mill bought ten power looms from John Midgley in 1839 for £100. Midgley had been the mechanic at Groves Mill until he moved to Wood Mill and then Wire Mill where he started making power looms in 1837. Robert Clough paid £8.25 for a 6 quarters loom from George Hattersley in 1841. Clough, and most early users, put them in their multi-storeyed mills before they learned that the vibration caused serious problems. William Lund & Son built the first worsted weaving shed in Yorkshire in Keighley at North Beck Mill in 1842. However, despite the local movement into power loom weaving, and as they were not employers of large numbers of hand loom weavers anyway, Marriners evidently came to the decision to stop that side of their activities and concentrate on spinning. Their first major extension of the mill premises in 1837 was a new spinning mill, not a weaving shed.[32]

## Labour

The Health and Morals of Apprentices Act of 1802 had little effect, apart from stopping night work for children, and a few years later the Factory Act of 1819 did not put into place any effective system for checking the use of under-age children or the hours of the under-sixteens. Other Acts followed in 1825 and 1831, but these were judged insufficient and pressure grew for a Ten Hours Bill. A Parliamentary Select Committee was set up with Michael Sadler, MP for Leeds as chairman. The Sadler Committee reported in 1832 and five of their witnesses came from Keighley. It should be noted however, that witnesses were chosen to strengthen the case of the reformers, were not under oath, and were often relating stories from their childhood. Twenty-seven year old Thomas Smith, who was then a weaver, had started work in a cotton mill at the age of six. He moved to Berry Smith's worsted Mill at Club Houses where he said they were not allowed to sit down during the 12¼ hour shifts and they were beaten if they appeared tired. He later had an accident by being caught in the shafting and left at eighteen to become a weaver working at home.

Samuel Rhodes started work for John Mitchell at Hope Mill, which was later taken over by Marriners. Six-year-old Rhodes worked long hours with harsh treatment from the overlookers who used straps with nails to beat the children. He felt that John Mitchell did not know what was happening at the mill. Hodgson's comment on John Mitchell was that he 'was a gentleman highly respected by his workpeople and the public generally, and what was better still, we believe a genuine Christian'. Rhodes went to work at a mill owned by Wilkinson, possibly William Wilkinson at South Street Mill, and then moved to Berry Smith's mill before becoming a wool comber for Thomas Bailey at South Street when he was fifteen.

Abraham Wildman, a warehouseman and wool sorter and Gillet Sharpe, Assistant Overseer to the Poor in Keighley, also gave evidence blaming the regime in the mills for all manner of ailments, deformities and the general ill-health of factory children compared with other children who did not work in the cotton and worsted mills. The last witness from Keighley was Joseph Firth, who was a worsted operative and said that a public meeting had been held in Keighley about the proposed Bill before Parliament. The parents of mill children who were there were unanimous in favour of the Bill.

Information given to the Factories Inquiry Commissioners provides an account of the labour force at Greengate Mill in 1834. Marriners were opposed to the introduction of the Ten Hours Bill which, they said, would be 'Ruinous to all parties'. The mill was run for seventy-two hours a week, depending on the supply of water to drive the 30 h.p. water wheel, their sole source of power. The mill hands worked from six in the morning until seven in the evening with a break for dinner from twelve to one. At other meal times food was brought for the children by their parents and this was eaten while they were tending the machinery.

In 1833 Marriners employed 97 people, thirty men and boys and sixty-seven women and girls. Their ages and wages were are shown in Table 4.5.[33]

| Table 4.5. Employees at Greengate Mill, 1833 | | |
|---|---|---|
| | *Males* | *Females* |
| Under 10 | 4 | 7 |
| 10 and under 12 | 5 | 8 |
| 12 and under 14 | 7 | 7 |
| 14 and under 16 | 6 | 10 |
| 16 and under 18 | — | 14 |
| 18 and under 21 | — | 7 |
| 21 and upwards | 8 | 14 |
| **Total** | **30** | **67** |
| | *Standing weekly wages* | |
| Under 10 | 2s. 0d. | 1s. 8¾d. |
| 10 and under 12 | 2s. 2½d. | 2s. 10¼d. |
| 12 and under 14 | 3s. 0d. | 3s. 5¼d. |
| 14 and under 16 | 5s. 0d. | 4s. 4½d. |
| 16 and under 18 | — | 5s. 7¾d. |
| 18 and under 21 | — | 6s. 0d. |
| 21 and over | 16s. 1¼d. | 5s.7½d |

There were also three females over 18 who earned 6s. 0d. (30p) a week on piecework.

By comparison, when a new manager for the heald yarn department was taken on in March 1835 his wages were £1 2s. 0d. a week with a house provided free of charge.

If the number of employees can be taken as a rough indication of the size of a firm comparisons can be made between Marriners and other Keighley concerns. Marriners employed 97 people in 1833 and they did not use the full amount of space at Greengate Mill as part was let out. Even so they were the second largest firm, in terms of employees, with only William Sugden at

# Green-Gate Mill Forfeit Sick Club.

### Established, January 25, 1832.

The Annual Meeting of the above Society, was held on Thursday the 25th Day of January, 1838, when a deputation from each Room was present. The Rules having been Read and the Cash Account examined, it was unanimously agreed, that, the observance of the Rules had been the means of preventing many little grievances which previously existed.

It was also resolved that the Accounts should be printed and a copy given to each Family, so that the Children as well as their Parents, might see how the funds arising from the fines, gifts, and subscriptions, are disposed of.

The following is a statement of money Received and Paid from July 1836, to December 1837, inclusive.

| DR. | Accounts of Monies Received for Fines, Donations, and Subscriptions, and to whom Paid. | | | | CR. |
|---|---|---|---|---|---|
| 1836, July 2nd | | £. s. D. | | | £. s. D. / £. s. D. |
| | Balance on hand from last account, .... 0 8 8½ | | Low Room. | Robert Smith, ............ 0 5 8 | |
| | | | | Esther Bradley, .......... 0 6 6 | |
| | Amount of Money Received } from Low Room, } | 0 8 10 | | Sarah Bradley, .......... 0 10 6 | |
| | | | | Barbery Eastwood, ...... 0 10 2 | |
| | | | | Caty Mehi, ............,.... 0 3 0 | 1 15 10 |
| | ——— from Washing Room, 0 4 1½ | | Third Room. | George Hartley, .......... 0 3 6 | |
| | | | | John Hartley, ............ 0 1 0 | |
| | ——— from Second Room, 0 0 3 | | | Hannah Smith, ............ 0 1 0 | |
| | | | | John Smith, ............... 0 2 0 | |
| | ——— from Third Room, .. 0 8 11 | | | Richard Ridehalgh, ...... 0 3 0 | 0 10 6 |
| | ——— from Fourth Room, 1 0 9½ | | Fourth Room. | M. A. Collingham, ...... 0 1 0 | |
| | | | | Susannah Clapham, ...... 0 8 1½ | |
| | ——— from Fifth Room, .. 0 11 10½ | | | James Stell, ... ... ... 0 1 0 | |
| | | | | Maria Bland, ............ 0 2 0 | 0 12 1½ |
| | ——— from New End, .... 0' 1 10 | | Fifth Room. | Sarah Ramsden, .......... 0 2 0 | |
| | | | | Maria Heap, ............ 0 7 7 | |
| | ——— from Dressing Room 0 4 10½ | | | S. Ann Wild, ............. 0 5 0 | |
| | ——— from Mechanics' Shop 0 1 5½ | | | Mary Greenwood, ........ 0 6 6 | |
| | | | | Margaret Greenwood, .... 0 0 6 | |
| | ——— from Warehouse, .... 0 13 8 | | | Susannah Totty, ......... 0 1 0 | |
| | | | | Betty Bottomley, ........ 0 3 0 | |
| | Donations, ...................... 0 19 6 | | | Sophia Greenwood, ...... 0 6 0 | 1 11 7 |
| | Subscriptions from Counting House, .. 0 19 0 | | | Balance on hand, Dec. 1837, | 1 13 9½ |
| | £6 3 10 | | | | £6 3 10 |
| 1838, Jan. 1st. | Balance on hand, .................. 1 13 9½ | | | 22 Persons has been relieved, of whom, 5 are dead. | |

N. B. For the further encouragement of the strict observance of the Rules, the Employers have agreed to double their subscriptions. Committee, &c, for the present year.—John Horne, Joseph Holt, Joshua Heap, John Heap, William Stell, and James Holmes   Spencer Booth Treasurer ———————— [CRABTREE PRINTER KEIGHLEY]

Mill Sick Club account for 1836.

Fleece Mill having more workers with 155 employed. Fleece Mill was built in 1820 and had a 12 hp steam engine as well as a 30 hp water wheel.

If accidents happened at the mill and medical attention was needed, Marriners paid the doctor's bill. When employees suffered other illnesses, help was provided from the funds of the 'Greengate Mill Forfeit Sick Club'. The funds for this club came from fines for lateness, neglect of duty, the wearing of ironed clogs in the mill and also from donations from the employers. The club was founded on 25 January 1832 and was run by a committee of workpeople, who paid to those in need.

This sick club survived until at least 1848 and possibly later. The use of fines received from the workers for such a sick club was not uncommon and it is interesting to note that Marriners also gave a subscription.

The Marriner brothers were also involved in charitable institutions in Keighley, which would have been of benefit to some of their employees. The firm was one of the eleven subscribers to the National School in 1822 when they gave £2 2s. od. The foundation of the Mechanics Institute on 14 February 1825 merited a subscription of £2 out of a total of £65 4s. od. This, one of the earliest institutes in the country, originated with four Keighley men suggesting that a society be established for mutual instruction and to support a library. They were John Farish, a reed maker; John Bradley, a painter; William Dixon, a painter and John Haigh, a joiner. By 1834 they had their own building which is shown on the poster on page 110 and later they moved to a larger building, which was on part of the present site of Keighley College. The original building was held under a lease of sixty years from the Duke of Burlington. Benjamin Marriner also acted as guarantor to the sum of £200 for William Sugden who was the treasurer of a savings bank founded by Benjamin in 1819.[34] This bank operated from a room at Greengate and was open from 12 noon to 2.00 p.m. on Wednesdays during the 1820s, but later moved to the Mechanics' Institute.

With the possible absence of any other bank in Keighley this would have been a useful facility for the townsfolk although it would seem to have been purely a savings bank. One person who took advantage of this bank was the Rev Patrick Bronte, the vicar of Haworth. In 1824 he wrote to Benjamin Marriner.

The daughter Patrick Bronte wished to send away to school was Emily, and she joined her three sisters at Cowan Bridge on 25 November. Other people mentioned in the letter are Benjamin's mother-in-law Clarissa Spencer and his wife Rebecca while the important personage was their baby daughter, Margaret. She was named after Benjamin's sister who was a friend and

---

## Mr Marriner, Worsted Manufacturer, Keighley

Haworth, near Keighley. Novbr 10th 1824

Dear Sir, I take this opportunity to give you notice that in the course of a fortnight it is my intention to draw about twenty pounds out of your savings bank. I am going to send another of my little girls to school, which at the first will cost me some little – but in the end I shall not loose [sic] – as I now keep two servants but am only to keep one elderly woman now, who, when my other little girl is at school – will be able to wait I think on my remaining children and myself.

Remember me very respectfully to Mrs. Spence [sic] and Mrs. Marriner, not forgetting another important personage, though younger and little.

Yours very respectfully. P. Bronte.[35]

---

confidant of the Rector of Keighley's sister, Isabelle Dury. The year before Isabelle had written to Margaret Marriner following rumours that she might marry Patrick Bronte who was recently widowed with six young children.

I think I never should be so very silly as to have the most distant idea of marrying anybody who had not some future, and six children into the bargain it is too ridiculous to imagine any truth in it ...

Benjamin and William Marriner were also Improvement Commissioners for Keighley and were thus concerned with the building of the gas works under the Improvement Act of 1824, and later, in 1831 the building of the court house for petty sessions. William Marriner was then appointed to the bench of magistrates.

CHAPTER FIVE

# Expansion and division, 1837–1888

THE FIFTY-YEAR PERIOD from 1837 until the break up of the firm in 1888 is, in some ways, more substantially documented than the previous years. The records are by no means complete however, for example, the type and quantity of machinery used are not covered. The records more or less terminate in the mid-1880's, before the split and dissolution of the partnership between Lister and Edward Marriner. Although Lister Marriner's branch of the firm continued in much the same form as before, and his son was able to buy back some buildings, almost no records have remained from either the late nineteenth or twentieth centuries. Also no records remain relating to Edward Marriner and the half of the assets he took at the dissolution.

The years between 1838 and 1888 saw very substantial changes in the West Riding worsted industry. Hand combing and hand loom weaving were finally replaced by combing machines and power-looms. The range of worsted fabrics greatly increased, as did the range of worsted and other yarns used in the manufacture of new varieties of fabrics for clothing and furnishings. Firms became more specialised and market forces favoured the development of the spinning side of the industry as compared with the weaving side. Large numbers of new mills were built to cope with the general expansion in demand, both at home and abroad. The development of these mills, together with the development of ancillary services such as engineering, commerce,

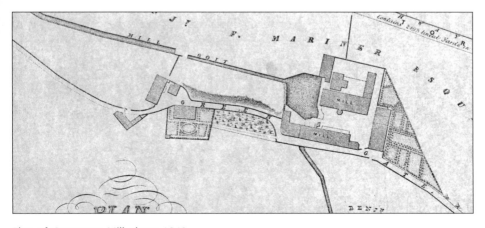

Plan of Greengate Mill about 1848.

transport and public services then led to the further development of West Riding towns such as Keighley.

From 1838 Marriners were concerned only with the processes up to, and including, spinning. The decision to specialise on yarn production enabled Marriners to diversify into different sections of the market for yarns. They produced two basic types of yarn; soft yarn such as hand knitting wool, and hard yarn such as heald yarn. They gradually moved away from producing yarn for weaving to specialise in hand-knitting, crocheting and machine-knitting yarns, although they still spun some warp yarns in the 1870s. Specialist yarns for fringes, braids and carpets were also produced. Most of their yarns were worsted, but mohair was possibly introduced in 1841, although it may just have been an experiment, as the company records do not show any mohair until 1871.

## Greengate Mill

The layout of the mill buildings can be seen from the plan of 1848. Water power was to remain important into the next century and the goit and the small dam are clearly shown. The water wheel was in the old mill, but steam was used to power the new mill and its various extensions, although they were linked with shafting under the yard. The old mill had gained two additions. These were a single-storey counting house by the gate into the mill yard, and several rooms at the other end with some used for storage and workshops with one rented out. The warehouse had some cottages attached to it at one end which were rented to employees. Entry to the mill yard was from Greengate Road, as it was then called. Greengate House was occupied at the time by William Marriner.

An illustration from 1850 for the firm's invoices and letterheads shows the

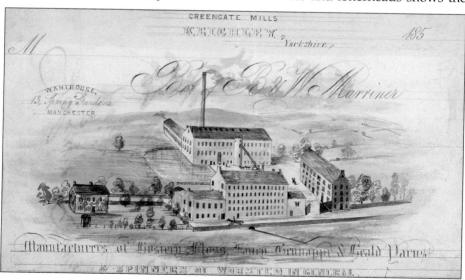

Greengate Mill about 1851.

old mill and warehouse with the new mill and chimney behind. There was now a high level bridge connecting the old and new mills. Although this is dated 1850 no significant changes had taken place since 1838. However, this extension of 1837 was to be the first of many, for as production increased during the next fifty years, more machinery had to be accommodated and more warehouse space provided. These later additions were made, not only in response to changes in demand, but also to changes in technology, for one of the processes, combing, was still a hand operation in 1838.

The stock book for 1838 lists the rooms in both old and new mills together with their use:

- Warehouse – this contained wool and yarn. (Yarn at Kidderminster and Manchester was also valued with this
- Low Room – used for slubbing, roving and carding
- Second Room – slubbing, drawing and roving
- Third Room – spinning
- Fourth Room – spinning
- Fifth Room – twisting and spinning
- Making-up room
- Fourth Store Room
- Third Store Room
- Thomas Waterhouse's Room
- Workshop – besides tools this also contained 'Moddles'
- Room over the water-wheel – governor
- New and Old Offices
- Engine House
- Drying House
- Wash House
- Middle Room
- Stairs – New clock, bell and ropes
- Spinning room – slubbing, roving and twisting
- Store Room
- Packing Room
- Dressing Room – for dressing heald yarn
- Boiling and Scouring Room
- Other Rooms in Warehouse
- Comb Shop at Greengate – 66 pairs of combs

This list shows that Marriners were still letting out room and power, this time to Thomas Waterhouse. He soon occupied more space than the list above

Mill bell.

indicates as he rented the middle room in the New Mill in 1839 and was supplied with power to run six spinning frames of 576 spindles and thirty-two power looms. For this he paid 4s. 3d. per spindle and £3 per loom per quarter, although the original rent suggested had been higher. Waterhouse was also allowed the use of a room for sizing and drying warps, but he had to put in his own steam pipes. In a later agreement, he rented a cottage and a room to put in six more power looms. These looms were to be put in before 1 May 1840 and the rent was on the same scale as before.[1]

The cottage Waterhouse agreed to rent in 1840 would have been one of six back-to-back dwellings built on the end of the warehouse and described in a letter referring to changes in mill accommodation which had affected the insurance policy for the mill in 1831. A comb shop and a store room had by then both been converted into cottages. These were next to four cottages of three storeys where the upper floors were used for storage. The letter stated that there were no combers on the premises, which would account for the 'Comb Shop at Greengate' with 66 pairs of combs mentioned in the stock book. Any charcoal-fired comb-pots would have been a fire hazard if they were too near to the mill or not separated in some way.

The total premises, together with machinery and some stock, were valued at £6,500 in 1838 on which an insurance premium of £30 2s. 6d. was paid. The insurance policy tells us that Marriners were using water power and a steam engine with a linked system of shafting so that the two power sources could be used to supplement each other. Mill engineers often liked this as it gave a smooth delivery of power with few speed variations. They also had substantial premises which they were proud to illustrate on their invoices where they advertised themselves as manufacturers of hosiery, floss, fancy, llama and heald yarns and spinners of worsted in general.

One ragged piece of paper in the Marriner documents gives another valuation of the mill premises. This unfortunately is undated, but was probably prepared in the early 1840s. The writer gave the value of the mill in 1817 at the time when it was finally bought by the Marriners as £4,900. It was noted that additional buildings to the value of £2,492 14s. 3d. had been added and that £532 16s. 0d. had been spent on enlarging the warehouse and cottages. They had spent £1,274 on a steam engine and boilers and had managed to increase the power of the water wheel by 20 h.p. These sums, plus the depreciated value of the original 1784 building, would roughly agree with the insurance valuation.

This document does not specify whether the increase in power from the water-wheel was because of a replacement wheel or because of alterations to the water supply. Certainly over the years the goit was widened several times but there were constant disputes about the amounts of water let down the river by the other mills. The disputes were not always about quantity, for Marriners complained to Butterfield Brothers, who ran Prospect Mill upstream, that there had been tar in the water. However, the mill dam, which was upstream and on the other side of the river from the mill, was enlarged about 1844 or 1845. At the same time, the goit was widened to six feet and excavated to a depth of three feet seven inches so it is likely that this was done to coincide with the installation of a new water-wheel.

The River Worth with Greengate Mill Dam on the right.

## Water power

The last water wheel was taken out during the First World War and no details of earlier wheels exist but they were probably about the same dimensions. A plan of 1893 shows the wheel to have fitted across practically the whole width of the original 1784 mill. It was 24 feet in diameter and 12 feet wide, with the drive taken from the inside of the circumference of the wheel. The dimensions of the wheel were typical of an advanced type breast wheel, which would have been needed to run a large mill. In September 1836, before the steam engine was installed in the new mill, the main upright from the water wheel ran at $14\frac{1}{5}$ rpm, while the line shafting in the Low, Second and Third Rooms ran at $41\frac{9}{14}$, $48\frac{8}{19}$ and $47\frac{1}{4}$ rpm respectively. After the steam engine was installed another shaft was connected which ran under the mill yard to the new mill and was connected to the shafting there. A scrap of paper referring to water power dated 1853 gave the total power available as fifty-five horse power with the wheel generating twenty-five and the steam engine thirty horsepower.[2]

In 1853 the Bradford Waterworks authority was proposing to take water from the river Worth. This prompted Marriners to attend a meeting at the Devonshire Arms in Keighley on Tuesday 17 May to oppose the plans. Marriners still depended on the river Worth for a good deal of their motive power and therefore the member of the family who attended the meeting collected some figures for their side of the argument.

Two estimates of the amount of water used by Greengate Mill were noted. The first was provided by Peter Barrett of Eastburn, an engineer who specialised in water wheels and water power. His father had installed a water wheel for Marriners and his son was to install another in 1882. They were a Sutton family who founded Eastburn Foundry and moved to a site near Eastburn Bridge. Barrett's estimate of what the water wheel would take was 13,996,800 gallons in 12 hours. However, the mill engineer's estimate of what water they were taking was 20,204,640 gallons in 12 hours, which shows a fair measure of disagreement! Whatever the volume of water used it produced 25 horsepower compared with the steam engine's 30 horsepower. The exception was after heavy rainfall when the wheel could yield 40 horsepower and give a consequent 'saving of coals'.

The Worth Valley mill owners successfully defeated the Bradford proposals so Marriners paid £71 for extra land to widen the goit once more and, in November 1859, paid Bailley & Mitchell, contractors, £336 for the work.[3] The supply was still inadequate so negotiations were opened with the Greenwoods for the purchase of the water supply to Broach Mill, a small mill on a tributary of the river Worth. Benjamin Marriner offered £400 for two acres of land, £100 for two old cottages and £450 for the exclusive rights to the water. This supply was taken over in 1867, a step which probably avoided the need to build a new reservoir. Isaac Booth, a surveyor from Halifax, had been at the mill in August 1866 to look over suitable ground at Ginger Bread Clough for a new dam, but this dam was never built. Booth regularly worked as a surveyor for Marriners.

Further expense was incurred after the supply of water to Broach Mill had been bought. The water had to be piped to Greengate Mill and Clapham Brothers, who were iron founders at Greengate in Keighley, charged £431 for supplying and laying the pipes and providing a gauge house in the mill yard. Claphams also had to provide railings round part of the mill dam. Samuel Clapham had started his working life working for the mill mechanic at Greengate Mill and one of his sons was also an apprentice for Marriners. Samuel was a strong Baptist and was baptised in Marriner's Mill dam while his mother lived in a house owned by the Marriners.

Maintenance of the water supply system to Greengate Mill was a constant expense. In 1869 the dam was cleaned out at a cost of £41 17s. 6d. and in the next year Claphams had to provide palisades for round the dam. John Bailey received £101 for repairing and cleaning the goit in 1871. In the next year enclosing part of the watercourse and straightening a footpath at Broach Mill cost £152. Later, in 1884, repairing the dam stones and re-walling the sides cost a further £327.

This expense was on top of the cost of a new water wheel, which was installed in 1882. In all the total cost of replacement was £1,061 with only £25 allowed for the old wheel. The cost was spread over three years and represents both the making and installation of the wheel together with the

removal of the old one. The new wheel, which was made by John Barrett of Eastburn, prompted a celebration, which was recorded by a small newspaper cutting in the Marriner archives dated Friday 11 August 1882:

> Trial of a New Water-Wheel. The trial of a new water-wheel at Greengate Mills on Saturday was made the occasion of a convivial meeting of the foremen employed by the firm of Messrs Marriner. The men assembled about six o'clock, and at half-past the water was turned on to the wheel by one of the sons of the firm amidst loud applause of those assembled. The wheel, which is capable of discharging 130 tons of water per minute has been successfully constructed by Mr John Barrett of Eastburn, on the most approved principles, and for the fall will be one of the most powerful water-wheels on the River Worth. After the wheel had been thoroughly tested in various ways, the party adjourned to the dining room attached to the mills, and under the presidency of Mr William Pickles, spent the evening in a most social and enjoyable manner. Mr Barrett, in wishing prosperity to the firm and success to his work, stated that eighty years ago his grandfather had put in the old wheel for the late Mr Marriner, and it afforded him very great satisfaction that the construction of the new wheel had been entrusted to him, hoping that in future, as in the past, his grandson might have the honour of putting in another wheel for the Marriners of the future. The party broke shortly before eleven o'clock.[4]

## Steam power

This faith in the position of water as an important and reliable driving force for the mill no doubt owed something to Marriners unfortunate experiences with steam engines. The original 30 h.p. engine from Haigh Foundry in Wigan needed attention from Cole, Marchent & Co, the Bradford engine builders, in 1859 at a cost of £228. The next year Gledhill & Dixon, iron founders of

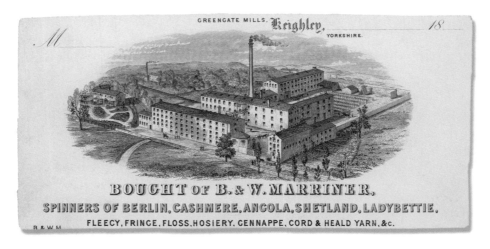

Greengate Mill about 1862.

Pollit & Wigzell engine plate from Greengate Mill.

Leeds, provided a new flywheel for £108. In 1862 Cole Marchent & Co were back with another wheel and attempts to increase the engine speed. The following year saw Green's Patent fuel economiser added at a cost of £201.

The mounting cost probably persuaded Marriners to replace their original engine as they obtained quotations from Bracewell & Griffiths (Late J Marsland & Son), Iron Works, Burnley for a new engine.[5] This firm offered to supply them with a beam condensing engine for £400 or a horizontal for £360. In a letter of 15 July 1865 bearing this quotation they said that their foreman engineer could go to Keighley to answer queries about the room needed for the engine and, when Marriners had decided which engine they wanted, would send a more detailed specification. This question of room may have been important, as Marriners probably wanted to use the existing engine house. On 19 July Bracewell & Griffiths sent another quotation for a smaller engine with an 18 foot flywheel costing, in all, £330, and added that they were hoping for the order.

This order was not forthcoming for Marriners bought a second-hand 40 hp beam engine from Clapham Brothers. This engine gave a great deal of trouble over the years. A new engine bed had to be laid in 1867. The stone cost £54 with an extra £81 to lay the bed, then an additional £241 to Cole, Merchant & Co. for repairing the engine in the same year. In 1872 a 'little engine' was installed. This was bought from John Yates for £272 and was probably used for auxiliary power for money was spent each year until 1875 repairing the other engine. In 1875 it finally broke and production would have stopped if Marriners had not hired a mobile traction engine or locomotive to supply

power. They had to pay James Boulton £100 a month for the hire of this engine in addition to £95 13s. 2d. in running expenses. This finally persuaded them to order a new engine from Timothy Bates & Co. of Sowerby Bridge, even though it did entail spending £479 on alterations to the engine house. The cost of this new horizontal engine, together with installation, amounted to £1,225. Even this did not stop further expense, for Pollit & Wigzell, who took over the business from Timothy Bates at this time, carried out £600 worth of alterations to the engine in 1882. A photograph of the Pollit & Wigzell plate which was fixed to the engine is shown on page 85. This new engine had a 60" stroke with a 19" high-pressure cylinder and 36" low-pressure cylinder but the old flywheel was used. The new steam engine had therefore been installed at the same time as the new water wheel.

A second engine house was built in 1889 after the partition of the firm. This was because the section of the mill then owned by Edward Marriner, Benjamin's youngest son, was served by the water-wheel and he needed to supplement this power. When the firm was partially reunited after Edward sold out in 1912, this second engine house was not included but the original 1784 water powered mill was returned. The mill was electrified in 1932 with Metropolitan Vickers equipment.

## New buildings

To cope with growing sales it was necessary to buy more machinery and also to expand the mill premises. The 1860s and 1870s saw a period of considerable expansion at Greengate Mill with the original 1784 mill becoming

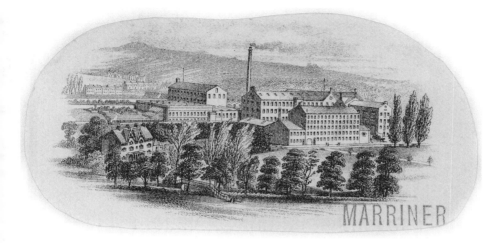

Greengate Mill about 1870.

a small part of a complex of buildings as land was bought for expansion. In 1860 a new warehouse was built for which Clapham Brothers provided a new boiler and hot water apparatus. In January the following year Sugden & Smith, architects of Cook Lane in Keighley, prepared drawings for an extension which would link together the new mill and the cottages attached to the warehouse. This extension cost £844, while rebuilding and re-slating the cottages cost a further £201. The year 1864 saw the addition of a new suds pond, with a new shed and combing room the following year. Clapham Brothers again supplied the ironwork in the form of pillars for the shed. In 1868 another new shed for the production of genappe yarn was built at a cost of over £2,000. This increased the demand for combed wool so another combing shed was added in 1868. The mill yard was then extended to provide more room for wagons and in 1870 a new oil and soap warehouse was built.

Oil and soap were necessary for the scouring and preparation of the wool so large quantities had to be bought and stored. The main supplier during the 1860s and 1870s was the firm of T & H Briscoll of 38 Mill Hill, Leeds. At times Marriners bought over £2,000 worth a year from them. Other firms supplied oil and soap from time to time, but only if they could offer a price advantage.

After the washing processes the soap, oil and grease from the wool were recovered as brown grease in the suds pond and grease works. This grease was then sold, chiefly to S C Lister, woolcombers of Bradford. However, in November 1873, B R Vickers of Leeds wrote to Marriners asking about this brown grease. Marriners agreed to sell them several tons at £16 a ton for they had 10 to 12 tons in stock. In return Marriners bought two chests of London refined cord soap at £2 3s. 0d. (£2.15) each. As production increased so did the amount of grease produced and a new grease works was built in 1872 at a cost of over £800.

In the same year a large new combing shed was built on Victoria Street at a cost of about £5,000. This was built onto the side of an extension at the

back of the new mill and covered the largest area of any of the mill buildings.
It was completed in 1873 when the shafting for power was carried through
at a cost of £146. Much of the new combing machinery was bought from
Taylor, Wordsworth & Co. of Leeds.

To provide accommodation for mill workers six cottages had been built at
Worth Terrace in 1869 and a further nine were added in Victoria Place in
1873. More additions were made to the mill premises with a new dry house
in the old mill in 1874 together with a new hoist in the old warehouse. The
higher level of activity necessitated new offices in 1876.

The mill buildings of 1878 are shown on the plan on page 91. This was
the point of maximum expansion for Greengate Mill. The mill chimney was
now at the centre of a complex of buildings built during the previous century.
The old water powered mill which had been built for spinning cotton, was
now a small part of a range of buildings producing a wide range of worsted
yarns for sale both at home and abroad.

## Machinery and equipment

In 1838 Marriners still relied on hand combing and had 34 pairs of 3 pitch
combs valued at 10s. od. (50p) per pair and 32 pairs of 4 pitch combs valued
at 15s. od. (75p) per pair. These no doubt would be used in their own comb
shop at Greengate. Besides having combers to comb their own wool Marriners
must have had wool combed away from the mill as it was not possible to
supply the number of spindles they had from the work of 66 hand combers.

Combing was still mainly done by hand at Greengate Mill until the 1850s.
In 1847 they had 28 pairs of 3 pitch combs and 34 pairs of 4 pitch combs
which were valued at 8s. od. (40p) and 12s. od. (60p) per pair. However, in
1854 new combing machines were introduced and the last stage of worsted
production to be mechanised was brought into the mill. The fact that payments
were made to S C Lister & Co. of Bradford suggests that they initially bought
Lister 'Nip' combs. Marriners continued to make payments to Listers during
the 1850s and 1860s but, as we will see later, they also had Noble combs.

After Marriners started machine combing they expanded that section of
their production several times. As we have seen, new combing sheds were
built in 1868 and 1872. Eventually they even extended into commission combing where they combed other firms' wool, particularly after the extension
of 1872 was completed. In the first six months of 1874 they received £32 from
James Clapham, £36 from Hughill Brothers and £19 from Benjamin Bedford,
all textile manufacturers in Keighley. They also received £224 from a number
of other firms for commission combing in the same period.

Marriner's charges for combing were explained in a letter to Benjamin
Bedford of Hope Mill, one of the customers listed above. Hope Mill is shown
next to Greengate Mill on page 123.

All long wools combed on Noble's combing machine will be charged 2d per lb
and if on Lister's machine 1¾d per lb, if backwashed ¼d per lb extra. Short
wools will be charged according to the tear they yield, 10 lbs top or more 2¼d

per lb. Wools sent to comb must be accompanied by *written instructions* which will be strictly adhered to.[6]

Benjamin Bedford paid Marriners £563, £632 and £728 for commission combing in the three years from 1874 to 1876. After that he had less wool combed and eventually had to give up his lease at Hope Mill. This was taken over by Lister Marriner in about 1880.

Following combing, the tops were carded and the building of the new mill in 1836 provided room for a new card which was bought in 1838. This would match the carding capacity to the new spinning frames. Marriners then owned four 'carding engines' as they were described in the stock record. By 1847 they were running eight cards, which is an indication of the increase in the amount of wool they were using. Taylor, Wordsworth & Co. of Leeds may have made some of these cards, for some years earlier they had quoted Marriners for the supply of a 'Carding Engine without box'. They had also quoted for a screw gill, a machine which was described by Hodgson as ... one of the greatest improvements in connection with worsted spinning that has ever been brought out. The advantage of the screw gill was that it helped to produce a much more even and firmer thread.

In 1838 the final spinning process was carried out on a mixture of old and new machines. Benjamin Berry & Sons of Lady Well Works, Hall Lane, Bradford, had offered new spinning frames at 14s. 0d. (70p) per spindle but these were refused. Instead four old frames of 66 spindles each were bought from Berry & Sons at a cost of 2s. (10p) per spindle later in the year. These were not the cheapest for Marriners were running a 72-spindle frame which they valued at only £3, or 6d. a spindle. Most of their frames were valued at more than that, however, although many were several years old and therefore had been written down in value. It was also still possible for Marriners to repair or possibly build their own frames for they had 245 spindles and flyers in the workshop.

In 1850 there were seventeen spinning mills in Keighley with an average of 1,684 spindles each. As Marriners had 4,216 spindles in 1838 Greengate Mill must have been one of the largest in the town. John Foster's new mill at Black Dyke in Queensbury outside Bradford, had 3,036 in the same year. That was also above average in spinning capacity for in the townships comprising Bradford Borough the 71 spinning firms had an average of only 2,325 spindles each in 1839. Although Greengate Mill held a larger-than-average number of spindles the number of spindles per frame was only 88. This compares with the average of 96 for the firms in Bradford and 105 for Black Dyke Mill. The reason was that many of the spinning frames in Greengate Mill were old and therefore smaller than the more modern frames. Some were twenty years' old and those smaller frames only had 74 spindles each. By comparison three new frames which Marriners made in their own workshop in 1836 had an average of 179 spindles each.

Possibly the main reason for the above average size of Greengate Mill in terms of spinning capacity in 1838 was that it was solely concerned with spinning. Many firms had installed power looms in their mills by that time although there was some fear of opposition from hand loom weavers in Keighley. For instance William Lund at North Beck Mill bought two worsted power looms in 1831 but did not dare use them for two years. Timothy Hird of Acres Mill hid his first looms among the spinning frames in 1834, but within a short time a good number of Keighley firms bought power looms. These initially were worked in the mill and therefore took up some of the space before single-storey weaving sheds were built alongside.

The decision by Marriners not to take up power loom weaving but specialise in yarn production necessitated a variety of types of preparing and spinning frames, for example special twisting frames for heald yarn. Unfortunately there are no specific records relating to the expansion of spinning in the years up to 1888. The valuation of machinery which was made at the end of each year from 1842 to 1884, does show however, that in certain years the stock of machinery was increased. For example, between 1873 and 1874 it went up from £7,841 to £10,050. The new machinery in the combing shed that had just been built can probably account this for. Marriners wrote to their Dublin agent in May 1874 saying ... We have just put down and have now got into working order an entirely new combing plant on the latest principles.

Apart from a few examples, evidence of the type and quantity of machinery bought and used is very scarce for a fifty-year period. What is known is that Marriners bought extensively from the local machine makers, particularly William Smith & Sons of Keighley and Taylor, Wordsworth & Co. of Leeds. On the other hand, they were never averse to a second-hand bargain if it was available. One example of this comes from a letter from Benjamin Marriner, who was in Leicester, to his son Lister.

## My Dear Lister                                    17 July 1853

I got safe to Keyworth (?) at 12.00 met Wm Sunderland (their Leicester agent) and walked to Touch Mills all alone. When I arrived they were selling lot 35 a long spinning frame which was taken by Jno Home at 2/4 per spindle and caused some difference among the jobbers.

The bidders consisted of 4 brokers from Bradford, 2 from Halifax and several Leics spinners, also R Martindale from Leeming of Manchester. He came to buy the 48 in card which was sold to Whelsdon for £200. I bid up to £160 but saw no chance. JH told me they intended to have £250 for it but the difference which had arisen about the spinning frame prevented him bidding. The frames that R Robinson asked me to buy for him went at twice the amount he fixed, everything that has been made by Smiths or Taylor, Wadsworth has sold very high and all to the Leicester spinners. Several of them made their acquaintance with me and wondered I did not bid. I have bought nothing today but will look sharp after them tomorrow.

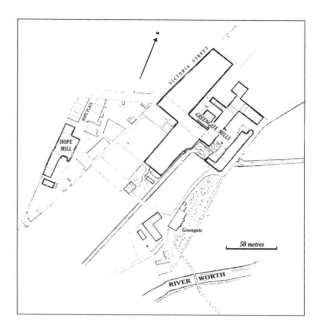

Plan of Greengate and Hope
Mills about 1878.

One process, which Marriners did not carry out themselves, was dyeing. The wool was put out to some of the local firms, for instance the firm of Oates, Ingham & Sons of Greengate, Keighley and Valley Road, Bradford, who dyed most of Marriner's yarns during the 1860s. Later Marriners tried several other firms of dyers such as I Robson & Sons of Bradford and Huddersfield and H Walshaw of Halifax.

## Wool purchases

Wool purchases increased considerably after 1842. The increase was not uniform as purchases were made on the basis of market expectations and these fluctuated during this period as in any other. The general trend though was one of expansion until the early 1870s when the West Riding worsted industry entered into the so-called 'Great Depression' which lasted until the 1890s.

It has already been seen how Marriners began to buy wool from the Bradford and Leeds merchants by 1828 or possibly earlier.[7] This practice continued and may have accounted for the greater part of the wool Marriners used. However, there is evidence of wool still being bought from farmers or dealers in the wool producing areas until the 1870s. William Lister Marriner went to the areas around Ipswich and Norwich to buy wool in 1866. Later, in 1874, wool was bought from Newbury in Berkshire. In this case Marriners argued about the cost of the wool and wanted to pay ¼d. per pound less than the asking price of 1s. 6½s. (8p) per pound. Their reason was that in their opinion … Demands of the trade *do not* warrant the late advance in wools. However, they must have thought that it was a good price for they paid the money promptly in cash.

Marriners did not use much foreign wool and therefore it was always possible to go to the farmers at shearing time and bargain for the fleeces. In doing so they by-passed the merchants, but had to pay in cash. They could buy at a lower price, but lost the advantage of buying on credit and possibly turning the wool into yarn for sale before they had to pay for it.

When cash transactions with farmers did take place they did not appear in the end of year lists of money owed by B & W Marriner. These lists of liabilities and assets compiled by Marriner's book-keeper showed the firms they owed money to and firms who owed them money. From these lists it is possible to see which merchants were dealt with, together with some estimate of the scale of the transactions. In 1842 Marriners owed £4,057 to twenty-five firms. Some of the sums were small but the significant ones were owed to Leeds and Bradford wool-staplers. The list of firms owed £50 and above by Marriners is as follows:

| Table 5.1. Trade debts over £50 in 1842 | | | |
|---|---|---|---|
| R Goodman & Son | Wool stapler | Bradford | £885 |
| William Marten | Wool stapler | Bradford | £577 |
| William Cheesebrough | Wool stapler | Bradford | £479 |
| John Wade & Co. | Wool stapler | Leeds | £275 |
| James Hubbard & Son | Wool stapler | Bradford | £263 |
| William Scholefield | Wool stapler | Leeds | £198 |
| J N Balme | Wool stapler | Bradford | £183 |
| Peckover & Co. | Wool stapler | Bradford | £113 |
| Hustler & Co. | Wool stapler | Bradford | £72 |
| David Bateman | Card maker | Bradford | £256 |
| William Smith & Sons | Textile machinery | Keighley | £247 |
| John Sturges & Co. | Bowling Iron Works | Bradford | £174 |

The number of wool-staplers on this list shows that Marriners bought from a variety of firms and this continued to be their normal practice. The sums of money outstanding are an indication of the scale of wool purchases and also of the usual three-month credit system allowed by the staplers.[8]

Lists for 1852, 1862, 1872 and 1882 show a similar but reduced range of debts, mainly to wool merchants, but also to textile machinery makers such as William Smith & Sons of Keighley, who supplied spinning frames.

The reason for the reduction in the number of names on the lists after the 1850s and the smaller amounts outstanding was that the credit system between wool suppliers and spinners changed. Wool-staplers usually granted credit to the spinners who then gave credit to the weaving firms who were their customers.[9] The cloth then went to the merchants on credit who in turn gave this facility to their customers. As the amount of money owed by Marriners on current transactions reduced it would seem that their wool purchases were initially financed by credit. Raw materials would have been the largest item for them to finance. The decline in trade debt after 1857 may have been due to an increase in direct trade with woolgrowers but this is unlikely. Possibly the main reason for the decline in the use of credit by Marriners was that the wool merchants would not provide this facility. The general financial crisis of 1857 may have led Marriners to turn to their bank in the absence of trade credit and certainly there is evidence of increased bank borrowing after 1870.

## Yarn sales

Information about where Marriners sold their yarns and how successful they were is very scarce. The general picture is of sales being conducted through three channels. First through agents, who sold on commission in Manchester, Leicester, Preston and Dublin, and for a short while in Glasgow and Kilmarnock. Secondly to merchants who specialised in the types of yarn that Marriners were producing. Finally they also sold some yarn directly to customers who used it for various purposes.

Throughout the period 1838–1888 Marriners were active in a number of yarn markets. Besides heald yarn they also produced hosiery yarn, which was sold mainly to the Leicester knitting firms, fringe and braid yarn which went to upholstery merchants in London and elsewhere, Berlin wool and floss yarn which were used for embroidery and crochet work, a wide range of hand knitting wools and some special yarns for the cloth trade such as fleecy yarns used for linings and Andalusian which was used for fine dress goods. Other types of yarn were produced at certain times including such varieties as cashmere and mohair.

Heald yarn, which had been produced for some years, was accounted for separately by Marriners. This yarn was used in the healds of looms for weaving wool, cotton flax and silk until late in the century. It was then replaced by varnished cotton yarn, which was cheaper and longer lasting. In December 1839 Moorehouse & Elliot of 69 Church Street, Manchester wrote to Marriners asking for two dozen of number 24 four-fold heald yarn to be sent to them every month. Separate accounting for heald yarn customers such as this firm continued until 1841 when total sales for the year amounted to £1,841. This was less than the previous year when sales had been £2,554. Extracts from the ledgers for these two years still exist as eight quarterly statements. Several doubtful debts were hopefully carried forward each quarter together with the debts outstanding from the previous quarter.

In the first quarter of 1840 yarn was sold to twenty-six different firms and totalled £641. The thirteen most significant sales were to:

| | |
|---|---|
| Moorehouse & Pollitt, Stockport | |
|     Reed makers, heald knitters and shuttle manufacturers | £97 |
| William Wood, Wigan | |
|     Cotton spinner | £61 |
| Swainson, Birleys & Co., Preston | |
|     Cotton spinners and manufacturers | £47 |
| John Ramsden Jnr, Bradford | |
|     Reed and heald maker | £42 |
| John Burton, Middleton | |

| | |
|---|---:|
| Cotton spinner and manufacturer | £39 |
| James Oates, Armley, Leeds | |
| Gear and slay maker | £37 |
| Burrow & Higgin, Lancaster | |
| Cotton spinners and manufacturer | £34 |
| James Eckersley, Wigan | |
| Cotton spinner | £33 |
| Hargreaves & Co., Accrington | |
| Cotton spinners | £26 |
| A & N Thornley, Hyde, Cheshire | |
| Cotton spinners and manufacturers | £22 |
| James Hyde & Sons, Duckinfield, Cheshire | |
| Cotton spinners and manufacturers | £22 |
| Mercer & Anderton, Clitheroe | |
| Cotton spinners and manufacturers | £21 |
| Henry Ledgard, Bramley, Leeds | |
| Gear and slay maker | £21 |

In the following year for the same period the sales over £20 were to the following firms:

| | |
|---|---:|
| John Ramsden Jnr, Bradford | |
| Reed and heald maker | £74 |
| James Oates, Armley, Leeds | |
| Gear and slay maker | £66 |
| William Barrow, Huddersfield | |
| Slay and heald maker | £60 |
| William Wood, Bradford | |
| Reed and heald maker | £46 |
| John Leach, Stalybridge, Cheshire | |
| Cotton spinner and manufacturer | £42 |
| Bannister, Eccles & Co., Blackburn | |
| Cotton manufacturers | £36 |
| William Wood, Wigan | |
| Cotton spinner | £31 |
| James Pollett, Holmfirth | |
| Heald and reed maker | £27 |
| Henry Ledgard, Bramley, Leeds | |
| Gear and slay maker | £26 |
| John Burton, Middleton | |
| Cotton spinner and manufacturer | £23 |
| James Hargreaves & Son, Kirkstall, Leeds | |
| Woollen manufacturer and merchant | £23 |

Horrocks & Jackson, Preston
    Cotton spinners and manufacturers           £22

The figures for these two periods show sales divided between two types of firm. Those in the cotton areas needed heald yarn to repair or make up fresh healds for their looms. The other firms on the list were all concerned with making loom parts incorporating heald yarn. Usually they were described as reed and heald makers and some of them, for example Henry Ledgard of Bramley and James Oates of Armley, had been customers of Marriners for at least ten years. The odd one out was the firm of James Hargreaves, of Kirkstall near Leeds, who were woollen manufacturers and merchants. They probably needed the heald yarn for their looms in the same way as the cotton manufacturers.

The quarterly sales for heald yarn in 1840 and 1841 were:

|  | 1840 | 1841 |
|---|---|---|
| First quarter | £641 | £678 |
| Second quarter | £552 | £336 |
| Third quarter | £705 | £399 |
| Fourth quarter | £638 | £429 |

Heald yarn was sold by Marriners for many years after the 1840s, but there are few details about its relative importance to the firm.

## Agents

At times there were some changes from the general pattern of sales through agents, merchants and directly to customers. Occasionally Marriners ran one of the agencies themselves before a new agent was appointed. One of the agents was buying for overseas markets and had an agreement with Marriners with exclusive rights to sell Marriner's yarn in certain countries. Some overseas merchants later acted as agents as they sold on commission rather than paying for the yarn and taking it into their own stock.

From the accounts drawn up at the end of each year from 1842 to 1884 it is possible to see the changing pattern of trade through Marriner's agents. Manchester sales had already been in the hands of an agent as James Brown sold Marriner's yarns there from 1833. Brown continued to act as agent until 1847 when his name was replaced in the accounts with an entry for 'B & W Marriner, Manchester' which indicates that they took over responsibility for sales. This continued until 1859 when David Parkinson took over on 1 October. He had 2½% commission on sales, and worked from premises at 13 Spring Gardens. In 1861 Marriners were again without an agent, but they appointed James Shimwell to that position in 1862. He lasted only a year before Marriners resumed responsibility, this time until 1877, when Shimwell again took over as agent and was still there when the accounts finished in 1884.

Marriner's agents in Leicester worked from premises at 61 Belvoir Street.

Over a period of forty years they had two agents; Thomas Sunderland until 1869 and then Edward Errin. The trend of sales in the Leicester area was an increase until the mid-1860s and then a general decline. This market was important, however, as at times a quarter of Marriner's production was sold to the machine knitting industry.

The increase in sales to the Leicester area came when the possibility of applying steam power to the production of hosiery began to be seriously considered after 1850.[10] The increase in factories was slow, however, and even by 1874 the total number of factory workers was only a small proportion of all those engaged in the industry. One of Marriner's largest customers, I & R Morley, still had 3,000 framework knitters delivering to their Nottingham warehouse in 1900 despite the fact that they owned seven factories.[11] I & R Morley did not start factory production until 1866 and Allen, Solly & Co. of Arnold near Nottingham, one of the best-known firms in the trade and another important customer of Marriners, did not start factory production until the 1880s.[12] Thus, although factory production was increasing, the framework knitters used much of the yarn supplied by Marriners.

The system of trading in the knitting industry was such that the spinners were expected to grant nine months credit to the manufacturers. The cost of providing credit was spread throughout the trade as the spinners made allowances when pricing their yarn. How Marriners fared under this system is not clear. Leicester certainly came to be an important market for yarn during the 1850s and 1860s, but sales fell away during the 1870s and 1880s.

Marriner's yarn was sold in Ireland by the Dublin commission merchants and agents Johnston & Inglis of 7 and 8 Eustace Street, but details are available

Trademark used by B & W Marriner about 1880.

Business card presented by B &
W Marriner about 1880.

only for 1873 and 1874. Marriners may have started selling there in the 1840s
when their agents in Leicester, Preston and Kilmarnock, were appointed, but
there is no real evidence of sales in Ireland until 1859 when George Fowler
owed them £247 at the end of December.

Johnston & Inglis were paid 2% commission on their sales. During the
1870s yarn was sold to such firms as Pirn Brothers of William Street, Dublin,
who were wholesale and retail linen and woollen drapers, silk mercers,
hosiers, haberdashers and poplin manufacturers. Other customers in Ireland
were N Fry & Co, coach lace and Irish Linen manufacturers as well as tabinet
makers and linen drapers, Geoghegan & Co, silk mercers, and Richard
Atkinson & Co, poplin manufacturers to the Queen and the Prince of Wales.

The agent in Preston, Thomas Grime, acted for Marriners for at least
thirty-five years. His business address was 10 Wellington Terrace and he
seemed to be most successful during the 1850s and 1860s. Sales fell off during
the 1870s as they did in Manchester and Leicester. Agents were also appointed
in Kilmarnock and Glasgow, but the volume of sales proved to be too small
for them to continue for long.

## Merchants

In the years after 1836, when Marriners gave up weaving and concentrated
on yarn production, there were several changes in the location of the mer-
chanting firms which dealt with worsted yarn. The changes were associated

with the rise of Bradford as the headquarters of the firms of merchants dealing with both the home and export markets. The situation was outlined by Henry Forbes when he was referring to Bradford in the nineteenth century ... At the beginning of the present century, and indeed for a long time afterwards, the town contained few (if any) resident merchants. Hence the purchasers of worsted fabrics who were in the habit of attending the Piece Hall only once a week resided principally in Manchester and Leeds.

With the increasing importance of Bradford as the centre of a textile producing area, the merchants from Leeds and Manchester moved to Bradford in the 1850s. Additional acknowledgement of the rising importance of Bradford was the establishment there of merchant houses owned by foreigners, predominantly German. In 1861 more than 40% of Bradford worsted merchants had distinctively foreign names. The changes mentioned above show up in Marriner's accounts although there was the additional factor in that Marriners eventually started to sell to merchants in Germany and France. Edward Marriner was asked, by his uncle William, if he was prepared to go to Germany for a year or so when he left school in order to learn the language for business purposes, but there is no record that he did so,

From the lists of firms owing money to Marriners at the end of each ten-year period from 1844 to 1884 it can be seen how the foreign merchants became important, although probably by 1884 many members of the firms were only foreign in name.

| Table 5.2. Number of firms owing money to B & W Marriner | | | |
|---|---|---|---|
| Year | Foreign name | British name | Total |
| 1844 | 7 | 56 | 63 |
| 1854 | 11 | 38 | 49 |
| 1864 | 8 | 26 | 34 |
| 1874 | 1 | 32 | 45 |
| 1884 | 15 | 30 | 45 |

The list in 1844 included:
Birkbeck, Quitzow & Co., Bradford – yarn merchants
F Schwann, Leeds – merchant
P Passavant, Bradford – yarn merchant
G & W Oldenbourg
Reuss & Co., Bradford – yarn merchants
Burghardt & Co., Manchester and Bradford – merchants

Lists for subsequent years were similar and included many of the leading Bradford merchants.

## Knitting wool

Marriner's position in the knitting wool trade is best explained by one of their many letters replying to a request for yarn. This one was from N & I Bulcock of Clitheroe to whom Marriners replied ... We do not keep a stock of fingerings as we only make to order for the wholesale trade.

Firms usually wrote to Marriners enclosing a pattern of the yarn they wanted and at the same time asked for a price. At times Marriners did not have the particular wool on hand and as it would then have had to be spun and dyed they did not like supplying in less than 200lb lots. Despite this Marriners received many requests for samples of yarn. To a request from a German firm to act as their agent Marriners replied that they had an agreement with a firm in Bradford whereby that firm of merchants bought exclusively from Marriners and used every endeavour to push this branch of the trade.[13] The German agency had been interested in their 'fingerings' or hand knitting wool which the Bradford merchants C Moeller & Co. sold in Germany and elsewhere. A similar request to sell their yarn abroad came from one of the largest Bradford merchant houses. Marriners had to refuse this order as ... In respect to fingerings we find on reference to our agreement, that it would be a breach of honour to accept your orders although it may be for a district on the continent perhaps unknown to our customers.[14]

Having to refuse orders must have been disappointing to Marriners for there appeared to be strong competition in the yarn market. Potential purchasers were always writing for quotations to find the lowest price and established customers were always trying to get ½d or 1d deducted from Marriner's list prices. Marriners, on the other hand, were always trying to obtain the best possible price for their yarn, often using the cost of wool or the cost of dying as excuses for not lowering their price. They would, however, deduct small amounts for large orders and for well-established customers, although they would argue about ¼d. a pound if it was to their advantage.

Sometime in the early 1870s Marriners started to trade directly with European firms, although they also continued to sell to Bradford merchants dealing with European markets. As we have seen Marriners had an agreement about sales to Germany, but there must have been some limitations on this for in 1873 they were willing to sell yarn to the Silesian Knitted Goods Company of Leignitz in Prussia (now Legnica in Poland). In 1875 they paid to have their trademark registered in Germany and this development of trade appeared to continue, for after the dissolution of the firm in 1888, the section taken over by Edward Marriner had an agency in Chemnitz.[15] This town in Germany was a major centre for the manufacture of hosiery.

Large amounts of yarn were also sold in France and at least one of the firms dealt with, Rembaud, Thoral & Lestier of St Etienne, appeared to act on an agency basis. Marriners wrote to them in November 1873 saying – to induce orders you may quote 1d per lb less than last time. Unfortunately however, only snippets of information are available about European sales and it is impossible to estimate their importance to the firm. Marriners were certainly not alone in supplying European markets for John James, writing about Keighley in 1857 explained that ... A considerable quantity of worsted yarn is also spun here for export.

Another strand to Marriner's trade started in the 1870s when they started to buy mohair from C Waud & Co., of Bradford. There appeared to be a contract whereby Wauds supplied mohair whenever Marriners wanted it. This mohair was sent on bobbins and was later sold by Marriners to their own customers after further processing such as being genapped. At times the arrangement nearly foundered, as Wauds did not always supply yarn as quickly as Marriners required. Occasionally there were arguments about price. Marriners said that Mitchell Brothers of Bradford sold mohair cheaper and hoped that Wauds would lower their price. At times Marriners did buy from Mitchells if Wauds could not supply the yarn at the price or time required.

On 12 January 1875 Marriners wrote to John Foster & Son of Queensbury near Bradford for samples of 2/40, 2/50 and 2/60 pure mohair in both brown and white. They wanted this on bobbins and said that they could give a regular order. They wanted the lowest possible terms but were willing to pay for ½lb samples. Both Wauds and Mitchells were behind with deliveries at this time when Marriners were trying to satisfy the demands of their agents in France. On the following day Marriners wrote to Rembaud, Thoral & Lestier saying that they could send prices and samples of Foster's mohair and asked if their customers wanted it genapped. Marriners also wrote to Wauds saying that they were ... pestered to death for the 2/50s and threatened with all manner of claims for delay and added ... please don't let anyone else have a lb until our order is completed. However, when the samples of Foster's mohair were sent to France, Marriner's letter was not encouraging for they said that they were ... quite sure they won't please so well as what we are sending. Your clients however are the people to judge this and we would like their reports.

## Finance

The surviving accounts of the firm were made up twice yearly from 1842 to 1884 and entered in two ledgers. These two books, together with a third ledger which contains some of the private accounts of the partners from 1858 to 1884, as well as details of purchases and sales, provide enough information to indicate the progress of the firm during the years up to 1888. Some relevant information is missing, however, so care is needed in interpreting the surviving records.

The first book, for the period 1842 to 1853, has some entries for yarn sales to a number of customers in 1841. When these accounts had been balanced at the end of that year Marriner's book-keeper, Spencer Booth, used the book to prepare the six-monthly accounts for the firm. Several pages were taken up each time with detailed accounts of the sums owed, followed by lists of firms who, in turn, owed money to Marriners. The first lists therefore include many wool merchants and the second lists included Marriner's agents and the yarn merchants and other customers who bought their yarn. Details of Marriner's position with regard to their bank, Alcock & Co. are also given. In 1867 an additional account was opened with the Bradford Old Bank. The value of wool and yarn on hand was always given, as were the stocks of other materials such as oil, soap and coal that were necessary for production. The value of the mill buildings was omitted between 1843 and 1860 and the value of the steam engine, boilers and water wheel was not given until 1867.

The total capital employed increased unsteadily to a peak in the 1870s, but was decreasing in the 1880s. It should be remembered however, that a large proportion of the firm's capital was tied up in stocks of raw wool, wool being processed and yarn awaiting sale. This major part of the firm's circulating capital was generally financed with a bank overdraft and with the credit allowed by the wool merchants. The value of wool and yarn in stock therefore varied with actual and expected demand as it was always possible for Marriners to buy wool on credit or borrowed money.

If the value of wool and yarn in stock is deducted from the total capital of the firm in each year for the period from 1842 to 1884 a more reliable guide to the expansion of the firm emerges. Although the figures contain a certain amount of circulating capital they show a steady increase in fixed capital during the 1840s and 1850s. This is reflected in the value of the machinery, which increased steadily over this period. There was possibly some renewal or expansion in 1850 and 1856 as the total value of machinery increased in those years. The greatest expansion in mill buildings and machinery employed in them occurred during the 1860s and 1870s. During 1867 the mill premises were enlarged with the building of a new shed for genapping yarn and new machinery was bought from William Smith & Son of Keighley. Further expansion continued during the early 1870s, particularly with the building of a new combing shed in 1872. This phase of rapid expansion lasted only for about six years from 1867 to 1872. No further changes were then made to Greengate Mill until after 1888.

The range of profits and number of losses incurred by Marriners does not indicate a highly profitable firm. The figures were distorted to a certain extent however, by private withdrawals by various members of the Marriner family. These withdrawals were for the purchase of land or houses, the running costs of those houses and later, in Lister Marriner's case, to cover a debt incurred from his interest in a quarrying and brick-making firm where he was a partner with Enoch Tempest.[16] The quarries were outside Keighley at Wicken Cragg, Woodhouse and Whin Wood. Despite this use of the firm's resources for private expenditure, the profit and loss account does indicate the trading progress of the firm. From 1842 to 1851 profits were made in all years apart from 1845 and 1847. This period was said to be ... A cycle of three unprosperous years, including the railway mania of 1845 and the panic of 1847 (which) terminated its course with 1848.[17] The years 1849 and 1850, when high profits were made by Marriners, were also years of general prosperity for the worsted industry ... In truth, were a spinner or manufacturer of modern times to point out two years of consecutive good trade, he would undoubtedly select these two for steady lucrative business.[18]

Those profitable years, not surprisingly, are indicated by an increase in the amount of wool and yarn in stock at the mill. The optimism created in those two years and a further profitable year in 1851 may have had unpleasant results for at the end of 1852, a less good year, Marriners still had £21,558 worth of wool and yarn in hand. From the increase in their trade debt and also in their overdraft, which at £17,943 was the highest amount for ten years, it would seem that there had been some incautious wool buying. Although 1852 and 1853 were not unprosperous years for the industry Marriners made losses. As their losses were large compared with the total capital employed by the firm – in 1852 £1,054 to £31,567 and in 1853 £2,493 to £21,703 – a more cautionary attitude to stocks appeared. Indeed the value of stocks fell by half from December 1852 to December 1853 and did not rise above £20,000 again for another twelve years.

The partnership of the two brothers, Benjamin and William Marriner lasted until 1857. Their income was made up of interest on their capital, rent from the tenants of their mill cottages and profits made by the firm as well as the return on any private investments they had. They apparently did not charge the firm rent for the use of the mill buildings, nor did they pay themselves a salary. Unfortunately there are few records of any of these sums, or of the two partners withdrawals from the firm. It would seem from later practice that annual withdrawals bore little relation to nominal income. One reason was that expenditure on the partners' houses was charged to these accounts. It could include the cost of the houses, repairs and alterations, a new green-house, or in one case, the cost of a new footbridge over the river Worth to avoid a long walk to the mill.

After 1857 William Marriner received £1,000 a year, free of tax, until his death in 1876. Withdrawals by Benjamin Marriner, and later his two sons Lister and Edward, continued to exceed their income from interest and salaries of £500 a year which were paid to them from 1867 onwards. As their debts to the firm increased they were eventually written off by being charged to the firm as trade expenses. This meant that the profits or losses shown in the firm's ledgers were worked out after withdrawals, and sometimes pay-ments, by the partners. There is no way of checking the true profit or loss situation before 1873, but from that year, and until 1884, the real position was entered in pencil in the year-end account.

The periodic expansion of the firm was almost wholly self financed. Extensions to the mill and new machinery were paid for as items of current expenditure, but this was not such a burden as expansion was generally slow and spread over a number of years. If the value of wool and yarn is deducted from the total capital employed, the resulting figure shows only a slow rise in fixed capital from 1842 to 1866. The increase in 1867 was substantial, but motive power had not been included previously and that added £3,661. There was also an upward revaluation of the mill buildings and machinery, which added £2,402 and £1,781 in each case, although these figures probably include some additions to both buildings and machinery.

It would seem that despite the substantial withdrawals by members of the family there was also an element of rent which would have been paid to their accounts as well as their share of profits when these were made. In all it is likely that the various partners left a proportion of their yearly income in the firm and this money was used to finance expansion.

During the period between 1867 and 1876 when many additions were made to the mill there is some evidence that money was borrowed. For instance, Thomas Sunderland, who was Marriner's Leicester agent, lent the firm £1,000 at 5% interest in November 1866 and this was repaid two years later in October 1868.

One sign of the increased prosperity of Marriners by 1867 was that it was the first year they were in credit with their bank, Alcocks & Co. Normally this bank allowed Marriners an overdraft, which had averaged about £11,000 during the 1840s and 1850s. However, in 1861 the overdraft rose to £16,440 and continued at that higher level until June 1866 when it reached £22,488. The reason for the increase was probably a combination of extensions to the mill and machinery and consequent increased purchases of wool. These growing purchases, together with the associated sales reflect the increased productive capacity.[19]

| Table 5.3. Wool bought and yarn sold, 1861–67 | | |
|---|---|---|
| Date | Wool Bought (£) | Yarn Sold (£) |
| 1861 | 64,861 | 81,926 |
| 1862 | 73,882 | 85,079 |
| 1863 | 84,942 | 97,687 |
| 1864 | 99,233 | 123,252 |
| 1865 | 94,580 | 117,850 |
| 1866 | 84,233 | 112,879 |
| 1867 | 80,731 | 110,371 |

The amount of trade credit available was still limited after the general crisis of 1857 and although Marriner's total trade debt did rise from 1861 to 1866 it appears that they were turning to their bank for help to finance the expansion from 1861. However, after Marriner's overdraft reached £22,488 in June 1866 Alcock & Co. wrote asking them to reduce this debt. Marriners replied that they would do so and endeavour to keep it as low as possible.

By December 1866 the overdraft was reduced to £6,286 and a year later they were in credit for the first time ever to the sum of £2,625. Clearly the expansion in productive capacity had paid off. In 1867 Marriners opened another account, this time with the Bradford Old Bank where, in December 1867, they also had a credit balance, this time of £4,899. This credit position only lasted for four years and in 1871 Marriners again had a total overdraft at their two banks of £10,623. This sum eventually increased and reached £48,198 in 1879.

The gradual rise of debt during the 1840s and 1850s was reversed with the collapse of the long credit system in 1857. The upward trend recommenced in 1860, but this time it was probably not so much a reversion to longer credit terms on the part of the wool merchants, but a natural increase because Marriners were buying more wool. This would result in a larger debt outstanding at any one time. This trade debt had reached £5,116 in 1866, but in December the next year had fallen to £208.

Marriners made profits in every year from 1865 to 1872 and the level was higher than previously, but what must be borne in mind is that these profits were calculated after payments had been made for new buildings and machinery. Expansion had started in 1860 with a new warehouse and gathered force after 1865 until 1872 when the mill complex was more or less complete. It would seem that Marriners were financing their own expansion out of ploughed-back profits and that the healthy financial state of the firm in the 1860s did not show up as 'book' profits but rather as physical assets.

The expansion of Greengate Mill in the late 1860s and early 1870s was a typical response to the boom conditions which existed for the worsted industry at that time. The American Civil War, which created a shortage of cotton as a competing fibre, was followed by the Franco-Prussian War, which reduced the competition of France in the sale of all wool fabrics. The resulting increase in demand for worsted yarn can be seen in Marriner's sales figures. Their best year was 1864 when sales reached £123,252. This produced a good profit despite the fact that the price of wool had risen to the highest point for forty years. It also marked the onset of a higher level of activity at Greengate Mill. More wool was bought, more yarn was sold, and the increased sales financed the expansion of the firm and for some years provided a credit balance at the bank.

The run of Marriner's profits from 1864 to 1872 ended with a loss in 1873 following the completion of a major extension. During the years that followed there were more losses than profits and whether the firm was up or down varied from year to year. From about 1874 until the end of this account was the period of the 'Great Depression'. Trade conditions for the worsted industry were unsettled with few people able to explain the reason. Profits, if any, were low, but there was a high level of activity with most mills working full time and an increasing consumption of wool, alpaca and mohair.

Figures for Marriner's wool purchases stop in 1876 but from the details of wool and yarn on hand it would seem that the level of purchases reached in the early 1870s fell only slightly up to 1884. It is apparent, however, that bank overdraft rather than credit financed those purchases. Trade credit rose to its highest at £4,421 in 1879 which was also a year when stocks of wool and yarn were high at £58,481, but Marriner's bank overdraft also reached its highest point in that year of £48,198. Thus Marriners were relying to a very large extent on bank credit to finance their production. Similarly in 1884 wool and yarn worth £33,274 was held in stock, and the bank overdraft was £32,323. There was also a trade debt of £3,888 offset by a trade credit of £10,041.

There is very little information about the scale of production at Greengate Mill after 1876. From plans of the mill it is obvious that there was hardly any extension of the mill premises after 1872 until the division of the firm in 1888. The value of the machinery used in the mill was written down after 1876 and continued downwards until figures ceased in 1884. It would seem that there was no re-equipping during this period.

Sales again are an unknown quantity. The only obvious point that can be made is that at a time when many firms in the industry were failing Marriners survived. Total sales were still high in 1876 compared with previous years but details of types of yarn or markets sold in are missing excepting those served by Marriner's agents. Only Leicester, which accounted for 16% of sales in 1876, was of any importance. British yarn exports fell between 1875 and 1884 so Marriners may have been hit by the contraction in overseas markets.

There are no figures to indicate if that was so or if the decline can be related to their financial position.

## Labour

The location of Keighley between Bradford and the Lancashire cotton towns was as much an influence on labour relations as on technological progress. The following comment was made about Keighley ... Politically the town fell under the influence of Bradford, and most of the movements in Bradford were reflected in Keighley politics.[20] The fact that the town was on the direct route from Lancashire into Yorkshire was also important during the Plug Drawing Riots of 1842. These outside influences were additional to the basic situation that ... the business firms provided the foundation of all local social relations and the most important political problems centred around the relations between masters and men.[21]

Marriner's relations with their work-people can be judged from two documents, which have survived from the years 1842 and 1843. The first of these came from the mill owners' reaction to the riots and disturbances of 1842, which were later described by Hodgson:

About the year 1842 there occurred very serious riots in Lancashire and the West Riding of Yorkshire, which were called the plug drawing riots, in consequence of the misguided mob stopping the mills by taking out the plug which prevents the water from running out of the steam boiler. Those disturbances originated in a certain strike or turnout in some parts of Lancashire, being joined by a number of Chartists, who adopted as their battle-cry, the five points of what was called the people's charter, the agitation for which at that time, was exceedingly rife; though many of those misguided people scarcely knew what they were about, yet they seemed to agree in the sentiment that they would never return to work till the charter was granted. We recollect those rioters coming to Keighley; in the course of a few hours they succeeded in stopping all the mills in their onward progress through Lancashire, but besides stopping the mills, they demanded food from the inhabitants, and gathering strength as they went along, they became a formidable mob by the time they reached Yorkshire. At Halifax they were met by the military when the Riot Act was read, but for some time they refused to disperse, and only took to their heels after several of them were shot.

When, the day after, the mob visited this town, there was not a single Lancashire rioter to be seen in the neighbourhood, still there was a good deal of excitement amongst the people of the town, the magistrates took the precaution to swear in several hundreds of peaceable inhabitants of the town as special constables who had orders that, whenever they heard the alarm bell they were to assemble at the Court House. It was in the early part of the week when the rioters visited the town, but on the following Sunday the excitement was as great as ever.[22]

Hodgson then went on to describe how a report of a crowd gathering on

Lees Moor outside the town led to great excitement, and the assembly of the yeoman cavalry, special constables and townsfolk. They then marched out of town and 'attacked' a Primitive Methodist meeting which was being held on the moor.

Marriners, with other mill owners, were naturally worried about the riots and so their workers were asked to sign their names at the bottom of a specially printed document.

> We, the undersigned, peaceable and industrious Inhabitants of the Town and Neighbourhood do hereby declare (Our employers having, after the recent lawless proceedings of a body of strangers, come to the determination of recommencing the working of their Mills) that we will individually protect and defend their lives and property to the utmost of our power, and also that we will not join any riotous assembly for any purpose, but will steadly mind our work and eject any Intruders who may attempt to stop our employment.
>
> As witness our hands this 19th Day of August 1842

This was signed by fifty workpeople, eleven of them with a mark, but this was probably not the total workforce.

The plug drawing riots in Keighley appear not to have been the serious affair they were in other towns. Sir John Brigg, who was the nephew of Benjamin and William Marriner, said afterwards that ... The plug drawing really caused no serious alarm or ill-feeling in this district. His father advised the plug men, when they visited his mill, to withdraw the fire bars from the boiler to avoid being scalded when the plugs were withdrawn. In the end the engine-tenter removed the bars for them and the plugs were knocked out in safety. The men seemed to have a duty to perform and at Calversyke Mill, owned by the Briggs, at least did it without violence.

During the 1840s there was a great deal of working class agitation in Keighley, which at times centred on particular groups of workers. One such group were the wool-combers. They were suffering from lower wages brought about by a great increase in their numbers as unemployed hand loom weavers and Irish immigrants turned to this last remaining hand process for work. Some firms were also starting to install machine combs, which could comb the same amount of wool in one day as one hundred hand-combers.[23] There had been a history of disputes by wool-combers starting with the famous strike of 1825, which lasted for several months. There were further strikes in Keighley in 1843, 1846 and 1849 and from the first of these survives a poster, published by the strike committee, which shows Marriners in a favourable light.

The poster gives details of wages and the attempts by the combers to persuade the mill owners to give an increase in the price they paid for having their wool combed.

Although Marriners did not install new combing machines for another eleven years the situation for hand combers grew worse and their attempts to maintain their standard of living were defeated. A committee appointed

# TO THE
# CLERGY, GENTRY,
## SHOPKEEPERS,
### AND
# Inhabitants of Keighley
## GENERALLY.

*Fellow Townsmen and Neighbours,*

WE, the WOOLCOMBERS of KEIGHLEY and Vicinity, take the liberty of presenting the following facts to your notice, in the full confidence of your sympathy and support. You may perhaps be generally aware that our condition, as a body of working men, has been anything but prosperous for a considerable time back. Through the frequent *reductions in our wages, and alterations* in the *wool*, an excellent Comber has been only able to earn, on an average, about Eight or Nine Shillings per week when in full employment. As might naturally be supposed, since the late improvement in trade a wish has been manifested on our part, to raise the price of our labour some little, knowing, that unless we did so, the first depression again in trade would probably sink us lower than ever. On stating our wish to some of the Manufacturers, one very influential Firm, viz. MESSRS. MARRINER, agreed to our request in a very gentlemanly manner. Having so far succeeded, we thought it only reasonable to cause the advance to become general, and for that purpose we agreed to draw out the Men in the employ of MESSRS. LUND, WHITEHEAD, & WILLIAMSON, intending, as they were only amongst the smallest Firms in the Town, to support the Men ourselves during the strike, and thus avoid becoming burthensome to the Public. Judge, however, of our surprise, when to frustrate our intention, the bulk of the Manufacturers left work this Morning, before setting off to Bradford Market, that unless we resumed our work to-day, and gave up all attempts at an advance they would every one cease weighing out Wool to-morrow morning, and thus put an end to the strike by a general stoppage. In consequence of this threat, we have made bold to lay our case before the Public, hoping that they will give us their countenance and support. We are far from wishing to make invidious distinctions, but we must say, that at present we are very much surprised at the conduct of many of our Manufacturers. It is well known that a great portion of them are religious and liberal men—great advocates for Free Trade and the prosperity of the Working Class, yet the only men who appear wishful to listen to our claims are two individuals, both of them Tories, and, as a matter of course, quite illiberal. We therefore trust, Fellow Townsmen, that should necessity compel us to solicit your aid, we shall not appeal to you in vain. We have stated our case to you in as brief and plain a manner as possible, and rest quite assured that our cause cannot fail to meet your approval and support.

### BY ORDER OF THE COMMITTEE.

*Keighley, Aug. 24th, 1843.*

N. B. We have just heard that MR. CLAPHAM, of Stubbin Mill, who had promised to give the Advance after a Strike, has since retracted. We cannot refrain from expressing our sorrow at the intelligence, as we fully intended having at least one liberal and humane man amongst the many Liberals.

### R. AKED, PRINTER, KEIGHLEY.

to investigate the condition of the woolcombers in the Bradford area in 1845 found that:

there were then upwards of ten thousand woolcombers in the town of Bradford and neighbourhood, the major part of whom were compelled to make workshops of their sleeping apartments, and to live amidst the vapours of charcoal. Unable to pay the rent for a comfortable dwelling, a large number huddled together in one apartment, and this redered their situation still worse. That their physical well-being was neglected, the emaciated appearance of most, plainly betokened.[24]

Despite the sad experience of the woolcombers the Marriner brothers appeared to have had more sympathy with them than did other mill owners. It was later said that ... The firm have always borne a high character for probity and uprightness. The two brothers were noted for their liberal sub-scriptions to charities in the town and it was said that the good name of the firm was proved by the large number of workpeople who had remained with them over a long period. This was something that remained true in the twentieth century.

The relationships between the Marriners and their workpeople in later years have not been recorded. However, during the second half of the nineteenth century many social occasions were arranged for the mill workers. These often revolved round the activities of the mill band, which went on to achieve national success and eventually became Keighley Borough Band. One typical event was a fete ... to be given to the work people in the employ of Messrs B & W Marriner, Greengate, on Friday afternoon, 18 September 1857.[25] From the brass band assembling at three o'clock with games, tea, races, sports and balloons followed by a concert in the new warehouse, to a fireworks display, refreshments and more amusements later, the firm certainly provided plenty of entertainment.

## The Marriner family

The first William Marriner died in 1809. He left a widow who was to live for many more years, and two sons, Benjamin and William, aged fourteen and twelve. These two brothers took control of the firm in 1817 and their partnership lasted for forty years until 1857. Initially the influence of the two brothers cannot be seen separately except in circumstances where, for example, Benjamin ran the mill and William bought wool (see Chapter 3). It does seem however, that Benjamin, as the eldest son, took the dominant position and later, as William did not marry, it was anticipated that Benjamin's sons would in future years be running the mill.

### William Marriner

The second William Marriner lived in the family home, Greengate House, which was near the mill, until he built a new house, called Worthville, on the other side of the river. He moved there in 1852 and in the 1860s started to buy land and small farms on the outskirts of Keighley at Mount Pleasant and other areas. In 1857, at the age of sixty, he gave up control of his share of the firm in return for the sum of £1000 a year, free of taxes for a period of forty years. He then moved from Keighley to Southport. William appeared to play a lesser part than his brother in business and local affairs although he looked after the Bradford market and was a magistrate on the Keighley bench.

## Benjamin Marriner

Benjamin Marriner, like his father, was fortunate in a financial sense with his marriage. His wife, Rebecca Mary Ann Lister Spencer, was the daughter of David Spencer, a Keighley wool-stapler and worsted spinner, and Clarissa Spencer (nee Lister) from the Lister family of Frizinghall near Bradford. Clarissa inherited land and property at Frizinghall, which had belonged to the Listers from about 1650.[26] Besides the Frizinghall estate there was also land near Spalding in Lincolnshire. As her only son died at the age of three this property passed to her daughter Rebecca and so to Benjamin and the Marriner family. Today there is still a Marriner Drive in Frizinghall, which is part of Bradford. To retain the link between the families Lister became a family name and William Lister Marriner, Benjamin's eldest son, was always known by his second name.

Although it is not relevant to the history of the firm, a letter from the Rev Patrick Bronte to Mrs Marriner survives. The Marrriner family appear to have had close acquaintanceships with the clergy in both Keighley and Haworth as this letter indicates. Mrs Marriner (Benjamin's wife) must have asked Patrick Bronte for information about lodgings in Haworth. His reply refers to the rooms at Sexton House, next to the Sunday School, which had been occupied by his curate, the Rev Arthur Nicholls, before his marriage to Charlotte Bronte in 1854. Rev Nicholls had given up the lodgings a year or so previously when it looked as though Patrick Bronte would not agree to the marriage. He had therefore left Haworth and took up a curacy at Kirk Smeaton near Pontefract

A diary for 1835 gives details of one of Benjamin Marriner's visits to Spalding in connection with his wife's land holding there:

Letter from Rev Patrick Bronte to Mrs Rebecca Marriner.

| | |
|---|---|
| Monday 9 March | Left for Spalding. Night in Leeds at the Golden Lion |
| Tuesday 10 March | By railway to Selby. Fare 2/– |
| | By Packet to Hull, best cabin. 2/6 |
| | By Packet to Grimsby, best cabin. 1/6 |
| | By coach to Louth. 1/8 |
| | Stopped at the New Rain Deer, Market Place |
| Wednesday 11 March. | Left Louth at 1.00 p.m. by mail. Fare outside to Spalding 14/– Arrived at ½ past 6. |
| Thursday 12 March | Left Spalding by the Perseverance to Boston at 7. Fare 4/–. 16 miles. Stayed at Peacock Inn at ½ past 9 o'clock. |
| Friday 13 March | Left Boston at 6 by pillion. Fare from New Holland 10/–. Packet to Hull 6d. Arrived by ½ past 3. |
| Saturday 14 March | Left hull at 6 by coach to Leeds. Fare 9/6. A wet ride. Found all well at home at 7.00 p.m. Expenses to Lincolnshire £5.19.0. |

During the nineteenth century the Marriner family became firmly

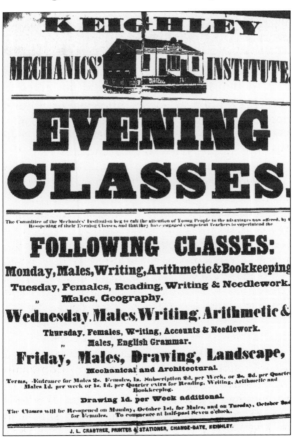

Evening classes advertised at the Mechanics' Institute about 1840.

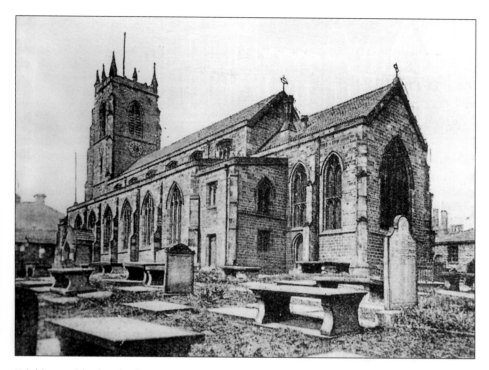

Keighley parish church about 1893.

established in Keighley. There were few political, social, municipal or cultural activities to which they did not lend their support in person or financially. When the Keighley Mechanics' Institute was established in 1825, the two Marriner brothers had membership numbers 98 and 99 and attended the dinner at the opening of the new building in January 1835. This interest in education was coupled with an interest in the church. Benjamin Marriner was a churchwarden and superintendent of the Parish Church Sunday School for forty-five years. The other teachers and scholars erected a stained-glass window in his memory. He and his brother William subscribed to the building of the new church and he was on the committee that dealt with the building arrangements. Keighley's new parish church was consecrated in 1848 when Benjamin's eldest son Lister, with his interest in music, organised and paid for the choir. Benjamin had close links with the clergymen in the area and there was correspondence between the family and, for instance, Patrick Bronte at Haworth.

Benjamin became a trustee of the Keighley and Bradford Turnpike Road and also of the Keighley and Halifax Turnpike. Both brothers were mentioned in the parliamentary bill for 1855–56 relating to the Blackburn and Addingham Turnpike with Benjamin becoming a trustee for the committee of the Eastern Division of that road. Both brothers had £50 shares in the Halifax, Bradford and Keighley Fire and Life Insurance Company. They also had shares in Keighley Market and took up new shares when it was extended in 1850.

Benjamin was also a trustee of the Keighley and Bingley Trustee Savings Bank in 1865.[27]

Following the Public Health Act of 1848, Haworth, and then Keighley, petitioned the General Board of Health for an enquiry. This was to examine the state of the town with regard to public health and to suggest improvements, which usually meant the setting up of a Local Board of Health. William Ranger, the inspector who reported on Keighley, found the usual squalid conditions which existed in most northern towns and recommended the setting up of a Local Board in 1854. Benjamin Marriner was one of the twenty-one members of this Board. A year earlier local people, fearful of cholera, had prepared the way by calling a meeting on 30 September at the Court House. Those present included the Board of Guardians, Board of Surveyors and the Improvement and Waterworks Companies and they debated ... *the purpose of deliberating and deciding upon the best means to be adopted for preventing, as far as possible, the introduction to or diffusion in the town and parish of Keighley of the Cholera or other infectious and dangerous diseases.*

With John Brigg (Marriner's brother-in-law) in the chair, ten resolutions were passed. The town was divided into districts with local supervisors. All streets, lanes, entries, yards, bye-ways and gutters were to be cleansed by removing filth and garbage and drains were to be purified. Dunghills, ash-pits, piggeries and privies were to be cleaned frequently and offensive smells were to be removed from workshops and farm premises. Most importantly ... if any attack of Cholera, or prenomitory symptoms, should come under the notice of any member of the Sanitary Committee, and the sufferer or friends be unable or unwilling to apply for prompt medical assistance, each member of the committee is empowered to supply the needful aid.

Both Benjamin and William were members of the Sanitary Committee. Benjamin, together with John Butterfield, John Clapham, Holmes Clapham and Thomas Paget was responsible for Utley, Utley-Green-Head and Spring Gardens area. William, together with Thomas Blakey, Joseph Craven, Joseph Firth, Joseph Keighley and William Shackleton was responsible for the Coney Lane, Low Bridge, Park Lane and Longlee areas. Large posters were put up throughout the town listing the resolutions and concluded:

> The Meeting has no wish to create alarm on the Cholera Subject, the complaint being now much better understood than formerly; mild cases are easily cured; and the worst cases not always fatal; nevertheless the prevalence of the disease in some parts of the country, and its fearful fatality, arising from ignorance or inattention, render it imperative on the part of the authorities, to adopt every known precautionary measure for the protection of the Inhabitants generally; and it may be stated, that, to working men in particular, fresh air, good water, plain food, dry and warm clothing, strict sobriety, regular sleep, and uniform personal and domestic cleanliness, appear to the Meeting indispensable to public safety; and the Meeting respectfully, but earnestly entreat the ready and vigorous co-operation of the Parishioners, in order that the measures indicated may be effectively carried out, and the disease, as far as possible, resisted or mitigated.

As we have seen above, fear of cholera and the poor social and sanitary conditions led to this action by the leading people in Keighley and was followed in 1854 by the establishment of a Local Board for Keighley.

A diary belonging to Benjamin Marriner when he was about forty, although not kept regularly, shows a busy man with many interests. There were visits to Manchester, trips to Leeds and Knaresborough to buy wool and payments to be made for rent to the Earl of Burlington. Many entries were to record personal and business transactions.

*1835*

| | |
|---|---|
| 19th January | A gas meeting at 11 o'clock |
| 21st January | Paid Wm & C Metcalfe £2.13.0 for Lister's half year schooling |
| 11th February | Lent John Ellison one German & 3 small flutes belonging to the National School Band. |
| 26th February | Paid tythe at Spalding |
| 21st March | Engaged Thos Bland of Cullingworth as manager of the Hd Yn in place of wm Pickles. Weekly wage of 22/– and also a house found by B & W M free of any charge to Thos Bland. |
| 3rd April | Otley Show day |
| 17th April | Good Friday. Opened new school at 7 o'clock this morning by a prayer meeting. Mr Drury read the 84th Psalm. |
| 19th April | First Sunday at the new school. Mr Drury gave an address. |
| 30th April | Lord Morpeth addressed the electors of Kly. |
| 2nd May | A journey to Skipton to oppose the constable being sworn in. |
| 27th July | School Feast. 655 scholars and teachers. 304 took tea at the tables." [28] |

In 1850 the roles of the family in relation to the management of Greengate Mill were laid out. By that time Benjamin Marriner had taken a more senior position while his eldest son, who was then twenty-five, had been given certain responsibilities. In addition the responsibilities of Spencer Booth, the firm's book-keeper, were set out.

| | |
|---|---|
| BFM | General Adviser |
| WM | Buy all wool and materials connected herewith. Sell Brook wools, Noils, Wastes etc. All yarns except those which already go through our agents, give directions thereto, and general correspondent. |
| WLM | General Inspector of the works and premises. Attend to yarn orders given in book etc. Ring first and last bell and see that all is strictly performed in its different departments. |

SBB    Keep and post all books, sell Heald Yarns. Collect accounts, pay wages and all other office departments.[29]

A few years later William Marriner retired from the firm and a new partnership was formed.

> Notice is hereby given that the partnership heretofore subsisting between us, the undersigned Benjamin Flesher Marriner and William Marriner of Keighley, in the County of York, Worsted Spinners, under the style or firm of 'B & W Marriner', was this day dissolved by mutual consent. Mr William Marriner retires from the business and all debts due, for and owing to the said co-partnership will be paid and received by the said Benjamin Flesher Marriner and Mr William Lister Marriner, by whom the business will be continued under the style or firm of 'B & W Marriner'.

Dated this 31st Day of July 1857       B F Marriner
                   Wm Marriner

Witness   Thomas Waterhouse, Solicitor, Keighley.

When Edward, the youngest of Benjamin Marriner's sons came of age, he, too, was given a position of responsibility in the firm. A new list of duties then had to be drawn and this probably dates from 1862 (when Edward was 21):

| | |
|---|---|
| BFM | General Inspector |
| WLM | Management of the Bradford Market |
| EDAM | General Manager of the machinery and charge of the execution of orders together with the Leicester and Manchester departments |
| William Naylor | Management of the books and of the occasional correspondence together with the Heald Yarn and Genappe Orders |
| Ellis Myers | Wages and calculations. [30] |

## Lister Marriner

Following the departure from the firm of William Marriner in 1857 and Benjamin's death in 1866, the business came under the control of Benjamin's eldest son Lister, and youngest son Edward. Lister was forty-one when his father died and already had considerable experience of the business. He had been a partner since 1857 and had worked in the firm for several years previously. Similarly, Edward Marriner, although 16 years younger, had been with the firm for some years. This meant that there was no abrupt change in the control of the firm when ownership shifted to the next generation.

Lister Marriner's diaries for the 1850s show a very active man with many interests. He went to Bradford twice a week to buy wool and sell yarn. Every few months he travelled further afield. For instance on 2 December 1851 he went to Lancashire to see the firm's Manchester agent, a Mr Parkinson, and also some of their customers. These were the entries in his diary:

Tuesday
Set off this morning by the first train for Preston. Finished business and staid all night. Mr Parkinson met me then we went to a lecture & called upon Mr Threlfall.

Wednesday
Visited all the factories in Blackburn, got well tired & on to Clitheroe in the evening. Spent it with Geo Beaumont, staid all night at Hothersalls, was much (...?) by my books.

Thursday
Got through Clitheroe & Accrington today & on to Burnley in the evening, where we staid all night

Friday: Wet and dirty
Round Burnley this morning. Mr Parkinson returned to Manchester. I came to Colne, then home; and spent the evening at Oaklands.

Besides his business interests Lister Marriner spent a great deal of time helping with the church, his brass band which he founded in 1845 and the military volunteers. These three, together with the mill, were all closely connected with his life. He married three times. His first wife, Martha, was the daughter of a local worsted manufacturer, William Anderton who ran Victoria Mill in Bingley. She died shortly after giving birth to their only child in 1852. When Lister and Martha had returned from their honeymoon after travelling to Leamington, Brighton, London and Morecambe, he noted in his diary that he met a Mr and Mrs Alston and their daughter. Five years after his first wife's death he married Elizabeth Alston, also a daughter of the 'Millocracy'. Her father was a partner in the firm of William Alston & Co, cotton spinners and manufacturers, of Merchant Street Mills, Blackburn. This time Lister's marriage produced eight children. After the death of his second wife in 1871, Lister Marriner married the daughter of a solicitor, Mary Butler. He then had four more children.

Lister Marriner and his brother Edward were as much involved in the development of Keighley as their father and uncle had been. Lister Marriner took a particular interest in the 35th Yorkshire West Riding Rifle Volunteers and rose from Lieutenant in 1860 to Captain in 1865 and Major in 1866.[31] Corps of Rifle Volunteers were set up in many towns throughout the country in 1859 to meet a military threat from France. They were organised county by county and their purpose was to

Lister Marriner.

be a national defence force available in the event of invasion. The Corps initially received little War Office funding so accommodation, uniform, arms and equipment were largely funded through subscriptions. Many local companies raised companies from their own workforces such as Joshua Tetley's brewery in Leeds and Akroyds of Halifax. Lister Marriner resigned his commission in 1868, but had been most active, particularly when he became commandant of the Keighley Corps. He had been instrumental in founding the corps in 1860 and had worked hard in raising money, recruiting and finding suitable drill premises. He persuaded the members of his band to join *en masse*, and in January 1861 they appeared for the first time in military uniform. He was not so successful with the appointment of drill sergeants, however, for they were men who liked the bottle and several had to be asked to resign after being drunk on parade. Lister Marriner was also a magistrate, but did not get involved in local politics in a public way although he was vice-president of the local Conservative Association at the time of his death.

Lister Marriner's great interest outside work was the church, particularly the Parish Church where he held many positions. In his younger days he was choirmaster and later became treasurer of the Keighley Church Sunday School Sick Society. He was on the commission established to deal with the restoration of the Parish Church and on a Bishop's Commission to re-adjust ecclesiastical boundaries. In 1872 a mission church was established near Greengate Mill to cope with the growing population of the town. This became St Peter's with the help of a subscription of £1,000 from the Duke of Devonshire and £500 from Lister Marriner.[32] His wife laid the foundation stone when the permanent church building was started in November 1880. He also supported the Methodist Sunday School near the mill, where the children of his workers attended. Although not a public man, Lister Marriner was a JP and member of numerous charity committees in the town. At one time he was vice-president of Keighley Northern Union Rugby Club and attended many matches.

### Edward Marriner

Edward Marriner was more obviously a public figure. He became Mayor of Keighley for the1885–86 year and served for nine years as an alderman, but before that he had been involved with many organisations in the town. One of his particular interests was further education and vocational training. In 1866 he was part of the group who supported resolutions passed by the committee of the Keighley Mechanics' Institute. These included:

> That a building be erected, suitable for the Institution, at a cost of from £6000 to £7000.

> That the proposed building shall include a Hall, Elementary Class Rooms, School of Art, Library, News Room, Club Room and Dwelling.

> That the following Gentlemen form a committee for carrying out the above resolutions, with power to add to their number.

Keighley Mechanics' Institute and Technical College 1893.

There followed a list that was a roll-call of Keighley mill owners and textile machinery manufacturers, including the two Marriner brothers. Edward himself later became treasurer and a trustee of the Institute while Lister Marriner's Brass Band played at the opening. The Duke of Devonshire opened the new Mechanics' Institute in 1870 with a large part of the £15,000 cost of the land, building and furniture being raised by public subscription. In the following year a Trade School was opened and within a few years Keighley became a pioneering town for technical education. Swire Smith, a local industrialist and several members of the committee of the Keighley Institute and Trade School, including Edward Marriner, undertook a fact-finding visit to France, Germany and Switzerland in 1872. British textile manufacturers were concerned at the time, as they have been ever since, about skill standards within the work-force and were facing increasing competition in Europe. This visit was to study the elementary and polytechnic schools there with particular attention being paid to the layout of buildings and their management. Swire Smith was later invited to represent the woollen industry as a member of a Royal Commission on Technical Instruction which produced a report in 1884 after visiting most manufacturing centres in Europe.

## Division

The brothers' record of public service was not, however, matched by harmonious personal relations. Lister and Edward Marriner quarrelled deeply and bitterly, to the serious detriment of the family business that had been built up over three generations. Throughout their dispute there ran an almost incredible streak of pettiness. Their quarrel, and ultimate division of the business, was a major set-back to its development at a crucial time within the industry. Later efforts to reunite the business by the repurchase of parts sold off were only partly successful and most buildings were never recovered.

It is not clear when the animosity between Lister and Edward started, but the first known argument began over payment for work done on their respective houses and the appropriate distribution of compensation when part of their land was sold to two railway companies. In the background, however, there was probably a basic personality clash and the struggle by the younger brother to gain parity with the elder. In addition, it has been suggested that Lister Marriner's son Henry, who was expected to take over his father's interest in the firm, was totally unsuited to business life and Edward resented his taking any role in the firm. Whatever the cause, the quarrel dragged on for over twenty years until even their solicitors grew tired of it.

Besides the mill and the old family home of Greengate House the Marriners owned other land and property. One of the houses was Worthville, which was built by William Marriner on land owned by the firm on the other side of the river Worth from Greengate Mill. By owning land on both sides of the valley, part of it was required when the two railway lines up the valley were planned. The first of these was the line from Keighley to Oxenhope, which was built by the Worth Valley Railway Company, now a private line. The Worth Valley Company paid £825 in 1865 for the land it required. The Worthville land was then regarded as part of the assets of the family which were not divided from their joint ownership of the firm. Later, when the Great Northern Railway Company wanted land for its Halifax, Thornton and Keighley line, Edward Marriner was living at Worthville and was not happy about money being paid for the land near the house going to his brother. The house itself belonged to Lister Marrriner, as he had inherited it from his uncle.

Discussion about the division of jointly held property must have been going on for some time, however, for Isaac Booth, a surveyor from Halifax was involved from at least 1876.[33] Booth wrote to Lister Marriner that year and gave his views on the subject:

> The whole of the mill premises at Greengate, your residence, together with cottages, land and Head Goit etc, as well as the new reservoir and land adjoining thereto, being so closely intermixed, and in fact being all so necessary for the convenient and profitable occupation of the mill as a manufacturing concern indicates the desirability of continuing them as one property and presents to my mind insuperable difficulties in the way of subdividing it.
>
> In a less degree this applies also to the property at Worthville and adjoining thereto, but I think that a sub-division of it, with a view to add to the completeness of Woodhouse and Worthville as separate Estates is comparatively easy but will simply require a great deal of care in the detailed arrangements.[34]

Edward Marriner had his own surveyor to look after his interests and the two brothers eventually communicated only through their solicitors.

Despite the references to division in 1876, nothing further was done until the problem of the land required by the Great Northern Company came up in 1880. This, and the need to carry out work at Worthville and Greengate House, brought matters to a head. A referee, Thomas Brook, a surveyor and valuer from Huddersfield, was brought in to give a decision as none could be arrived at in any other way. Originally Brook was appointed as the Marriner's surveyor in their dealings with the Great Northern. As the brothers could not agree about the ownership of the land the railway company wanted, Brook was asked to arbitrate between them.

The land in question had been bought originally by the firm on behalf of the partners. The firm's money had been used, but the land was regarded as belonging to the two brothers. Land for building Worthville had been taken and belonged to Lister Marriner. Another section further up the valley at Woodhouse belonged to Edward Marriner. The problem came with the payment for compulsory purchase by the railway company and the division, if any, of this money between the two brothers.

On 16 November 1882, at the Devonshire Hotel, Keighley, the arbitration court awarded Lister Marriner £2,216 for his land at Worthville which no doubt pleased him very much as the Great Northern had offered only £1,050. At the same place on the 17 January in the following year, Edward Marriner's claim for £1,578 for land at Woodhouse was not pursued when an offer was made in court of £1,000 plus 10% for compulsory purchase.

It is not clear if there were any problems regarding the division of these sums but to avoid further arguments Brook was asked to make a decision as to which parts of the estates should be regarded as essential for the running of the firm, and how the remainder should be shared out. In doing so he was bound to make judgements which were difficult for the brothers to accept. Lister Marriner wrote to Isaac Booth in 1884 complaining that he understood that Brook was preparing to let Edward have Greengate House. That would mean, he said ... the old homestead of the family to go to the youngest son. He added that Edward already had Broom House in Keighley with another house in Southport to come to him. Anyway, argued Lister, with his large family … I could not get my household into Worthville.

Brook made his award on 14 May 1885 and provided for a simple division of the property, which was not used for manufacturing purposes. However, he had taken on a task which was to prove pointless for, despite his earnest intentions to keep Greengate Mills intact as a going concern, the dislike between the brothers could not be lessened. The continuance of the firm of B & W Marriner meant that they still had to work together for their mutual benefit. This did not satisfy them so plans were made to dismember the firm.

Edward Marriner tried to find loopholes in Brook's award and this led to the appointment of another arbitrator, Samuel Jackson, an architect and surveyor from Bradford. A helping hand from a further third party, William Brigg of Calversyke Mill, who was the husband of the brother's sister, Sarah Jane Brigg, was refused by Lister Marriner for reasons explained in his reply to this letter:

March 15 1887

Dear Lister

I find today that there is just one chance of keeping the old firm of B & W M together. If you can put Harry (Lister's son Henry) into some other trade or to some other place – I think Edward would agree to go on as usual, and all the loss and trouble of dividing and starting the 2 concerns would be avoided – Just think it over, as it is the only way I see out of the trouble.

I am yours truly, Wm Brigg

16 March 1887

Dear Will

I duly received your note of yesterday and return you my thanks for your evident desire to conciliate matters between Edward and myself. The one chosen you refer to is altogether quite out of the question and seems to me that you do not quite understand the situation between us. Edward has insisted on a dissolution for several years past and when first suggested to me I confess that I could not then see that such a thing as a division of our Mill premises could be carried out but during the last two or three years various circumstances have intervened which have influenced my former views and I have after much careful consideration deemed it best to face the difficulty rather than continue as hereto. I have endeavoured to coincide with Edward's views all along and I have now agreed to his last proposition of dividing the buildings, to be legally conveyed so that we may each know our own: this I think is a very unwise step but I agree to it on the understanding that all be divided and with as little delay as possible for past experience proves to me that anything joint is most undesirable. Edward proposed that we should appoint an arbitrator and each prepare a scheme to be submitted to him.

Mine is ready and as you decline to take this matter in hand (for the reason you stated to me) I am agreed that Mr Saml Jackson, whom Edward proposed to value the property should continue to act for us rather than introduce another stranger into our affairs and I am now impatiently waiting to know if instructions have been given to him. It has ever been my wish to study to treat Edward in a straightforward and honourable manner and all I ask from him is that I may receive the same.

I remain, yours sincerely, W Lister Marriner

In November 1887 Lister Marriner was still urging all haste to Mr Jackson to draw up the dissolution agreement. Part of his reason may have been in his suggestion ... That no machinery be removed, taken down or sold prior to the date of dissolution except by mutual consent.

Jackson had suggested earlier that year that machinery in the mill should be moved so that two separate businesses could be established. One would deal with the hard or long wool trade, the other with the soft wool. The various buildings were to be specified as being used for these trades. He suggested that the old mill, new shed and part of the warehouse could be used for the soft trade whilst the new mill, wash house and other shed, with a share of the warehouse, could be used for the hard wool section. This division of building was similar to the one finally decided on, but both brothers carried on both branches of the trade when they took over their respective shares.

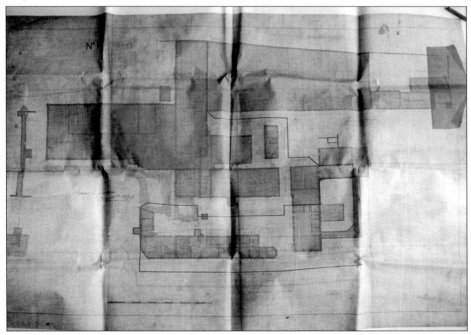

Samuel Jackson's drawing for the division of Greengate Mill, 1889.

The agreement to dissolve the partnership between William Lister Marriner and Edward Marriner was signed on 3 January 1888. Samuel Jackson was to settle and decide all questions which arose from the dissolution. At the end of the month two circulars were sent out to business contacts and others. The first under the name of the old firm:

1 February, 1888

Dear Sir

We beg to inform you that the partnership between Mr W L Marriner and Mr Edward D A Marriner in our firm has been this day dissolved by mutual consent under arrangements by which the Manufacture of Hard Yarns is taken over and continued by Mr W L Marriner and the Manufacture of Soft Yarns by Mr E D A Marriner both of whom will carry on business on their own account at Greengate Mills which have been divided for the purpose. Mr W L Marriner will carry on business under the style of Marriner, Son & Naylor and Mr E D A Mariner under the style of Edward Marriner & Co.

Yours obediently, B & W Marriner

The second circular shows how Lister Marriner had prepared to get round some of the difficulties in being left with only half of the mill premises as well as being cut off from the production of soft yarns. It is headed 'Greengate and Hope Mills' and gives the future intentions of his firm in a positive way. Unfortunately, if Edward Marrriner prepared a similar circular it has not survived.

31 January 1888

Referring to the circular sent to you by this post announcing the dissolution of the firm of B & W Marriner, Greengate Mills, Keighley, we beg to inform you that the business so many years conducted in that name will still be carried out *in all its branches*, at the above mills, by William Lister Marriner (Senior partner in the late firm), William Naylor (for many years interested in the late firm) and Henry Alston Marriner, under the style or firm of Marriner, Son & Naylor. Mohair, Alpaca and Worsted Genappes, Shetland, Andalusion, Berlin and Crewel Yarns, Knitting and Hosiery Yarns, in White, Natural, Drabs and Fancy Mixtures, will be produced as heretofor in all the well-known qualities.

Thanking you for the confidence reposed in the late firm, and soliciting a continuance of the same, we beg to draw your attention to the signature at foot, and remain,

Yours truly, Marriner, Son & Naylor

The dissolution of the partnership with the setting up of two separate firms did not end the dispute. There were problems of steam supply and the provision of power from the water wheel and steam engine that went on for several years. It was obviously very difficult and expensive to duplicate all the services required, but it had to be done. As Lister Marriner wrote to Jackson ... I cannot afford to run his machinery at a loss to myself. Lister

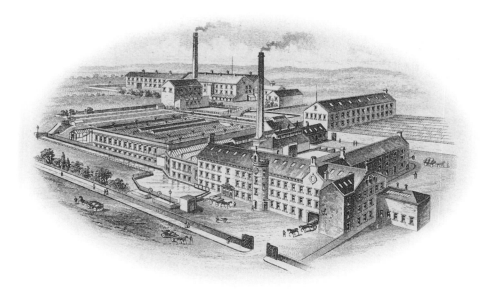

Greengate and Hope Mills about 1890. The sections of Greengate Mill taken by Edward Marriner have been omitted by the artist.

Marriner was given the 1836 mill and the attached warehouse together with the 1868 shed and the buildings in between. Edward took the original 1784 mill and old warehouse with the new combing shed built on Victoria Street. He needed to have his own steam engine installed, but insisted that shafting be provided to bring power from the water wheel round to his other buildings. This resulted in the building of a low L shaped structure, which ran from the warehouse to part of his mill. As this was something that had been allowed for under the original agreement the cost was borne equally. It seems that Edward was determined to make Lister pay for things that were not really necessary.

In the following years the links between the two firms became less. Steam and power became separate by 1890, but other problems remained. According to a letter to the two brothers dated December 1892 Samuel Jackson was hopeful of completing his award concerning the division of the mill premises in the following few days. However, he was still not happy about things.

> Can nothing even at this late hour be done to let the Greengate Mills Estate remain as one Estate? He went on ... I may add here that there has already been far too much money spent on dividing this estate into two parts. Never in my experience have I seen works done so grudgingly as I have to divide this Estate and so it will be to the end unless I am able in this my last effort to get you to see with the same eyes as I do. I know this business has been delayed for too

long, if it needs any excuse I may say the task has been a difficult one. Every time I have taken the matter up I have always felt that the money being spent upon the Division of this property was being done and is doing it, to reduce its value as a whole.

On my signing the award dividing this estate into two parts, it is my judgement that the reduced value will be completely effectual to an extent that can only be ascertained when the divided parts have to be dealt with in the way of sale.

By October 1893 the solicitors on both sides appeared to be rather tired of the situation as the first award had still not been made because of small differences. Killick, Hutton & Vint, the Bradford solicitors acting for Edward Marriner finished a letter to Wright Waterhouse, who represented Lister Marriner, with the following resigned statement ... *We have exhausted all our efforts to push the matter on and we have told our client that he must do what he can to expedite it himself.*

By 1898 the arguments had got round to who should hold the relevant deeds for the case. In the following year the partition deed was signed, but the correspondence went on for several years afterwards. In all the brothers came out roughly equal in the division of the property. In the absence of any data it is impossible to discover the effect of these events, but as has been suggested, they can scarcely have been conducive to profitable trading. Certainly, from the scale of the mill buildings prior to the division, it would seem that B & W Marriner would have been one of the leading firms in the area.

Edward Marriner & Co set up as spinners of Berlin, Cashmere, Shetland,

Trade mark of Marriner, Son & Naylor with MSN on the bow of the boat.

Andalusian, Fleecy, Fringe, Hosiery and Fingering Yarns. They kept the association with the family name by having 'Sailors' as their trade name. In 1893 *The Century's Progress* provided a very fulsome account of the business.

A thoroughly representative and responsible firm at Keighley, and one that has obtained its leading position by the uniform merit of the work it turns out, is that of Messrs Edward Marriner & Co of Greengate Mills, the well-known spinners of 'Marriner's Yarns', well know all the world over for its unequalled quality of, material, manufacture and durability. Up to 1888 Mr Edward Marrriner had been in partnership with his brother, Mr W L Marriner and on its dissolution took over this business on his own account. He brought to bear upon his new undertaking a thorough practical knowledge of every department of his speciality, together with good executive ability and sound business habits. His name has been identified with the manufacture of yarns for underclothing for many years. The premises are spacious in extent, and in every way fully adapted for the successful control of a business of this kind. They consist of wool warehouse, wool washing, combing, carding and drawing rooms etc on the ground floor, the equipment throughout being the result of the proprietor's long acquaintance with the business, and includes the most improved and best productions in wool combing, drawing, spinning, roving, reeling, twisting machinery etc, operated by steam-engines and water power. Two hundred and fifty hands are kept constantly employed in supplying the demands made upon the firm, and an efficient system of discipline and organisation is maintained in every department. The productions of the firm are recognised in the markets as standard goods and as having no superiors. The firm are also known as fancy spinners, and are largely occupied in the manufacture of Berlin, Cashmere, Shetland, Andalusian, fleecy, fringe, floss, hosiery, mending and fingering yarns. In these special lines they have few successful rivals. The material is obtained from the best sources of supply, prepared by efficient machinery, and every process is carried through under competent supervision. The firm are no less known for the quality and finish of their work than for the reasonable and moderate prices at which it is quoted. A leading speciality consists of hosiery yarn specially prepared for the wants of the Leicester and Nottingham districts. The connection acquired by the house is widespread and influential, attending to every part of the United Kingdom, and to the principal markets of the Continent. For the better control of the business agencies are in operation at Leicester, Glasgow, Brussels and Chemnitz in Germany. The telegraphic address of the house is 'Sailors, Keighley', and the telephone No 2219. Mr Edward Marriner is a popular and respected business man, strictly honourable in all his dealings, and commanding the confidence of all who come into business relationship with him. He is no less distinguished in the municipal than in the industrial life of the district, having creditably filled many of the principal public offices, and also noted for the active and practical interest he takes in all charitable and benevolent movements. Mr Marriner is ex-mayor of Keighley, a Justice of the Peace for the county, and an Alderman of the borough. He is also chairman of the Keighley Tramways Company.

So the situation continued until 1912 when Edward's part of Greengate Mills was put up for auction just two weeks before he died. It should be noted though, that the premises advertised were only about half of what Edward had received in 1888. The auction notice read;

The mill and premises known as Greengate Mills, Greengate, Keighley, lately occupied by Edward Marriner & Co, comprising Mill, five stories high, two warehouses, packing and store rooms, water wheel and gearing room, offices, mechanic's shop, dynamo rooms and oil stores, reservoir and goit together with the main and counter shafting, pulleys, drums, driving gear, gas, steam and water pipes, hoists and lifts.

The motive power is derived from a powerful water wheel and the lighting is provided by a dynamo driven by the water wheel.

The water rights are of an important and exceptional character, the reservoir, goits and mill dam providing a never failing and plentiful supply of water *which* may be utilised with great advantage for condensing and business purposes.

The area of this lot including the sites of the buildings, reservoir and goit is 21,100 square yards or thereabouts.[35]

In the meantime Lister Marriner had continued in business. About 1884 he had bought Hope Mill for £4100 so that when Greengate Mills were divided the new firm of Marriner, Son & Naylor was not restricted by losing property. Their notepaper showed Greengate and Hope Mills with a fair degree of artistic licence. The parts of Greengate Mills that had gone to Edward were left out so that the mill goit looked like a decorative water course and Hope Mill was made to look as though it was contiguous with Greengate Mill. A new trade mark was registered with the initials MS&N on the prow of the life-boat, which was used to retain the sea-going play on the family name.

Lister Marriner's partners were his son, Henry Alston Marriner and William

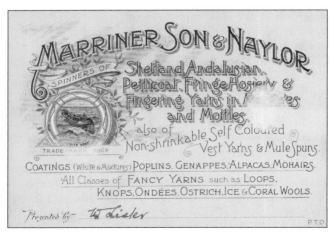

Marriner, Son & Naylor business card.

Naylor, who had been a manager with the old firm for many years. Henry was Lister's third son and Lister wanted him to join the company as his eldest son, William Herbert Lister Marriner, became a doctor. In 1888 Henry was twenty-seven and presumably worked for the firm for a few years, although he had little interest in it apart from the income it provided. His interests were the volunteers from which retired as a major in 1903 and the church choir where he was choirmaster for twenty years. William Naylor had been a junior partner for some time before 1888. He was a magistrate in Keighley and became a county councillor in 1889. Lister's second son Benjamin, who was destined for the church, had died in 1880 and his fourth son, who had worked in the mill for a short while, died in Africa in 1891.

Following the death of Lister Marriner in 1906, and William Naylor two years later, the firm took the name R V Marriner. This decision may have been taken by Lister Marriner's surviving children to ensure the future of the firm. Raymond Vincent Marriner was the eldest surviving son of Lister Marriner and his third wife. He had followed an electrical engineering training with the Brush Engineering Company in Loughborough and London and was a good business man. His elder half-brother, who had been a partner for several years, was uninterested in business and was reputed to have said that any firm should be able to support one gentleman, meaning himself. He was choirmaster at the Parish Church and spent most of his time at the mill composing sacred chants. Another brother, Norman, who was born in 1879, was expected to take a leading role within the firm but died at the age of twenty-three after only working in the firm for a few years. Little help could be expected from Raymond's other two brothers. Sidney had a career in the army and Kenneth was a surgeon. It was therefore left to Raymond to change career and return to Keighley and the family business.

After Raymond Marriner took control of the firm in 1908 it continued with his name until it was dissolved in 1995. Hope Mill was sold, but some of the premises which had been made over to Edward Marriner in 1888 were eventually bought back, mainly the original cotton mill of 1784. The large combing shed called Greengate Shed, built in 1872, together with the old warehouse at the side of the old mill yard had been sold and used by outside firms. Production was concentrated in the remaining buildings and the family then continued, with mixed fortunes, though the first half of the twentieth century.

In 1924 the firm became a private limited liability company, R V Marriner Ltd. Raymond Marriner was later assisted by his son, J R L Marriner, until the firm was sold to Union International Ltd in 1957.

Marriner

32
81

# CHAPTER SIX

# The last hundred years

H AND KNITTING, as a domestic activitiy for women, was encouraged
during the First World War when huge numbers of balaclava helmets,
scarves and socks were produced for the soldiers fighting in France and
elsewhere. Having acquired the skill, women continued hand knitting garments during the 1920s and 1930s with the additional incentive that hand
knitted garments became fashionable. Firms such as Patons & Baldwin started
to employ designers after the war and knitting leaflets became available for
a few pence. One famous designer was Anny Blatt who brought out a couturier
range of knitted suits and dresses. Women's magazines then followed with
designs and patterns for the home knitter. Competition between the magazines
led to them vying to present the latest trends in home knitting and knitted
wool separates became included in every woman's wardrobe. In 1932 the
first monthy magazine devoted mainly to knitting was produced and then
illustrated the latest trends in hand knitting. Casual clothes had arrived with
jumpers and cardigans being worn by most people, while Fair Isle and other
patterns became very popular.

At the end of 1920 Marriners decided to advertise in the trade journal, *The
Wool Record & Textile World*. They claimed to be spinners of all classes of
hosiery and hand-knitting yarns in botany and crossbred wools as well as
camel hair. These yarns were available on the home market or for export,
but they specialised in camel hair and wool mixed yarns for sports' coats,
cardigans and scarves.

During the 1914–18 war much of the yarn produced at Greengate Mill was
in khaki and navy blue for the forces and the mill would have been working
full time. However, by 1921 Greengate Mill was only working 16 hours a
week and lacked orders. This appeared to be the general situation in the
trade and there were said to be ... failures every day in Bradford. In April
that year Ray Marriner, and his twin brother Sidney Marriner, decided to
start selling hand knitting yarn by mail order. Sidney Marriner had been a
soldier for most of his life but joined Ray Marriner in the firm in 1919.[1] They
had dealt with a small company, which sold their yarns to retail shops, but
the man running it had got into difficulties and owed them £3,000. Some of
the stock intended for this outlet was left in a range of colours and so they
decided to sell it themselves as a way of recovering some of their loss. The
intention was to sell this stock by advertising in small local weekly newspapers
and, if sales proved worthwhile, to produce more of the same colours and

continue with the mail order trade. So as not to be seen to be cutting the price of Marriner's own yarns this new enterprise was to be run under the trading name of the Carlton Spinning Company. The intention was to sell yarns at 7s. 9d. (39p) per pound in weight, which would normally have retailed at 12s. 0d. (60p) in the knitting wool shops.[2]

In 1924 the decision was taken to convert Marriners into a limited liability company with a nominal capital of £30,000. At incorporation the purpose of the company was described as:

> To carry on the business of combing, spinning, doubling, weaving, knitting, manufacturing, or dealing in worsted, woollen, cotton, hair, flax, hemp, jute, linen, silk, or manufactured other fibrous substances and the preparation, dyeing, bleaching, mercerising, colouring, or finishing of any of the said substances and the buying or selling of yarns, cloth, or other fibrous substances.

Ten thousand cumulative preference shares at £1 and twenty thousand ordinary shares at £1 were available with the two subscribers being Ray Marriner and his wife Winifred.

In 1927 Ray Marriner was living at Mundens, High Spring Gardens, while his Uncle Henry still occupied the old house at Far Greengate. The firm were described as being spinners of Berlin, Cashmere, Shetland, Andalusian, hosiery and fingering yarns of all classes as well as camel hair.[3] Ray Marriner started his working life in the electrical industry and it may have been his experience that led to the decision to scrap the steam engine which drove the machinery in the mill. This was replaced with electric motors on each floor that still drove the machines through the existing line shafting system. Each machine still had its own belt and pulley as before. This change took place in 1932.

In the early 1920s negotiations opened with the directors of L Copley-Smith & Son Ltd who supplied knitting wool to the retail trade and had premises at Lower Mosley Street in Manchester. The idea was for Marriners to sell a good proportion of their yarn to Copleys. By March 1935 Copleys held 500 of the ordinary shares with the right to appoint directors one of them being George Copley-Smith. In March 1939 the directors of R V Marriner were Ray Marriner, his son John who had joined the firm in 1934, and Noel Copley-Smith. Winifred Marriner had retired and Noel Copley-Smith had taken over from George Copley-Smith. At this time Marriners were supplying Copley-

Yarn scouring in 1927.

Smith with about 80% of their yarns and much of their output was hand knitting wool. A small amount of yarn was sold through their shops in Keighley. One was on Halifax Road near the mill and the other was on Church Green near the centre of the town and near the market.

During much of the early 1930s about 200 people worked at Greengate Mill. Work started early at 6.00 o'clock with breaks for breakfast and lunch.

Copley's knitting pattern from about 1940.

During the week the mill stopped at 5.30 p.m., but Saturday was a half-day with the machinery stopping at 12.00 noon although the mill workers had to clean around the machines for another half hour before they could go home. The mill was organised in sections with most of the staff being women with male overlookers. Workers at the time found it a happy place to work compared with other mills and the Marriner family had a very

Marriner's knitting pattern from the 1950s.

paternalistic management style. Overlookers were not allowed to swear at female staff and labour relations appear to have been good.

During the Second World War Marriners ran with a depleted workforce and were subject to Government restrictions. They provided yarn for service clothing and then utility products with much yarn being exported. At the end of the war colours returned to normal and some yarn for moquette fabric was produced. In 1946 the decision was taken to develop the firm's own selling organisation as the agreement with Copley-Smith had been terminated. This was a considerable change as they had to employ their own team of travellers, as they were called then, to sell directly to the retail shops. To assist sales they started advertising extensively in ladies' magazines under their own name and brought out their own knitting patterns. They were the first firm to use colour photographs to illustrate these patterns and make them more attractive to the home knitters. Hand knitting was still a very popular pastime with special wool shops opening and department stores stocking a range of hand knitting yarns from different spinning firms. More designers were taken on and all the companies employed local knitters to try out the new patterns before they were issued. Competition between the various manufacturers was strong, as a successful pattern would result in increased sales of yarn. Patterns were produced, as they had been since the 1930s, for men, women and children using the brand name of the particular firm. Fashion for adults was changing with more informal clothes being worn which increased the demand for hand knitted garments. Men, for instance, would wear a sweater or cardigan where previously they would have worn a cloth jacket. To finance this new venture the share capital of the firm was doubled to £60,000 in 1949 with two members of the family who lived in Bournemouth taking up the additional shares. Two years later a mortgage was taken out to raise additional capital. By 1950 a large percentage of Marriner's yarn production was being exported. This was not done directly, but by using the traditional method of Bradford merchants. The number of processes carried out at Greengate were reduced. They no longer bought wool to sort and scour themselves and dyeing was also done elsewhere. They concentrated on drawing, spinning, twisting and reeling together with the final ticketing and inspection. However, the demand was such that they were running an additional shift in the evening in 1950 and employed nearly 300 people. In 1949 a letter was received from J & J McCallum Ltd, who were based at Leighpark Dyeworks in Paisley. The firm was a branch of the British Cotton and Wool Dyers' Association and suggested that a joint advertisement be prepared based on the connections between themselves and Marriners for the last hundred years.

During the 1950s the national consumption of wool rose and the market for hand knitting yarn also rose with firms such as Paton & Baldwins and Emu Wools reporting increases in sales.[4] Two reasons were put forward. The first was the heavy weight of the yarn used in the new 'quick knit' sweaters and other knitted garments. These patterns and yarns had been brought into fashion to make it quicker and easier for the unskilled knitter to knit a sweater or cardigan. The second was the introduction of the new home knitting

Part of the knitting wool inspection department in 1950.

machines which encouraged the use of larger quantities of yarn. These machines were hand operated but enabled a line of knitting to be completed in a few seconds although adjustments for length and design took longer. People bought these machines as knitted garments were still relatively expensive to buy in the shops.

Despite the favourable market conditions the family did not have the capital to re-equip or modernise their millI. Much of the machinery was old and the premises were even older. In addition, John Marriner did not have the same enthusiasm for business as his father, who was well past normal retirement age. The decision was taken to sell the firm as a going concern so, in 1957, The Union International Co. Ltd, owned principally by the Vestey family, bought the assets, good will and debts of R V Marriner Ltd and operations were merged with J P Heaton Ltd. Heatons were wool combers and spinners with premises at South Street, Keighley. At Low Mill they operated as wool combers and worsted spinners producing yarns for the moquette, hosiery and knitting trades.[5] Union International were meat importers from South America and their decision to buy the two Keighley firms was probably linked to the rising state of the wool market and the possibility of being able to use South American wool or even wool taken from the carcases of sheep killed for their meat. In addition this seemed an appropriate time to enter the textile industry as ... the industry has established new post-war records. Consumption of wool was at its highest point for seven years.[6] However, the value of the Marriner name was recognised, and the Marriner Wools label was retained for knitting yarns, with R V Marriner Ltd continuing as a separate company with directors appointed by Union International. John

Marriner was retained as manager to run Greengate Mill, which was used for the final processes of preparing hand-knitting yarn for retail sales. Union International staff knew little about the wool textile industry and relied heavily on their managers. They had to buy several companies to achieve the scale of operations they required and this, it is suggested, may have been the seed of their eventual downfall. An interlinking group of companies was formed based on J P Heaton Ltd. As well as Marriners there was Healey & Mathewman Ltd and another company, J W Allen Ltd which was set up to buy wool and prepare tops for Heatons. The original planned source of raw wool from the South American trade proved insufficient so J W Allen was needed to buy and comb additional supplies.

There appeared to be a rising market for knitting yarn and Union International's plans to control all the processes from the sheep to the final product were backed with considerable financial strength. They were not alone in their optimism as the chief designer of a rival firm commented in 1959 that:

> Casual clothes, an innovation in the 1920s, have become commonplace in the 1950s, and to-day a wool sweater can look equally smart on the race course at Ascot or at a cocktail party in Mayfair. In fact, it is an all-round-the-clock fashion theme, for there is no occasion in the domestic or social life of the modern woman when she need feel conspicuous because her hand-knitted clothes are out of place.[7]

John Marriner stayed with the firm for six years after 1957, but it would appear that a general decline in the wool textile industry and slackening of demand for hand knitting yarns brought losses to the new owners. Wool dropped by £1.00 per pound weight in the first year and despite the purchase of other companies the combined group was not large enough to compete with the market leaders. Losses were made in most years. In 1971 a loss of nearly £43,641 was reported with cumulative losses rising to over £500,000. Exports rose, reaching a maximum of £35,000 in 1974 but overall losses continued. In May 1973, John Marriner and his wife left Keighley for Southwold and the link between the Marriner family and Keighley was severed.

During the 1960s some new machinery was installed although much of it was old, some from the old firm of Hall & Stell of Keighley, with the name cast in the frame end. The drawing process was on the 'Bradford System' but the Raper Autoleveller system had been introduced because of its advantages in producing a more uniform product. Some old fly spinning frames were converted to spin mohair which was part of the range of yarns produced. A variety of yarns were spun to cater for different parts of the hand-knitting market. These ranged from the heavy yarns such as Aran for thick sweaters to fancy yarns with special effects such as a metallic thread or knarled yarn twisted in for more decorative ladies' wear. About a hundred people worked at Greengate Mill at the time. Eventually some of the spinning was transferred to Heatons with Marriners dealing with the later processes leading to balling and labelling.

On 28 October 1975 a fire started in the warehouse, which contained large stocks of hand knitting yarn already packed for the winter 'knitting season'. The fire spread slowly during the afternoon and not all the staff were aware

Advertisement for Marriner Wools near Knowle Mill.

of the seriousness of the situation. Office staff were asked to return and bring out office equipment such as typewriters and adding machines but in the rush the main fire-proof safe was left open and the firm's records were destroyed. The fire spread from the warehouse to the office block and the mill itself, despite the efforts of large numbers of fire fighters. Extensive use of wood in the old buildings, together with its absorbtion of oil over the years and the stocks of wool meant that the fire was fierce and devastating. Hundreds of spectators crowded the streets nearby, and on any rising ground that gave a good view point.

The fifty staff were evacuated as the fire took hold and extensive damage was caused to most of the mill buildings. The mill at the time was used for hand-knitting production, including balling, making-up and warehousing. Damage was estimated at £500,000 and the decision was taken to demolish the other buildings which had been saved from the fire, and so the original Greengate Mill of 1784/85 was pulled down. Some staff were moved to Heatons at Low Mills while others moved to Hope Mills which had been rented for storage purposes some time previously. Preparation of the hand knitting yarns was then moved to part of Knowle Mills on Halifax Road with the new address registered in March 1976. J P Heatons already occupied part of Knowle Mills and business continued, but at a lower level, and, for some reason, if an objection had not been received, the company would have been struck off the company register in 1978. The decline in sales of hand knitting yarns continued and in November 1983 negotiations were started to sell Marrriners with many of the staff working short time. The experiment with textiles by Union International ended and they reluctantly had to make the remaining staff redundant. It is not clear what happened to R V Marriner Ltd as a corporate entity. It is likely that the firm remained dormant after 1983, although there were some problems with creditors in 1991, with the firm being finally dissolved on 12 December 1995.[8]

A company owned by Robert Feather and Ted Arnold bought some of the assets of the firm and moved them to Parkside Mills in Pitt Street, Keighley.[9] The two partners used an existing company, Toprobin Ltd, changed the name to Darnis Developments Ltd in January 1983 and then to Marriner Yarns Ltd in June that year with the firm incorporated in August. A clause had been added to the company memorandum to enable it to trade in textiles in June, and the original registered office was in Bradford. Ted Arnold already had experience of the hand-knitting markets and was a director of A & P Wools Ltd, Universal Wools Ltd, and Knitters World (Wholesale) Ltd. The registered office was moved to Parkside Mills in 1984 and the share capital was increased to £30,000. Yarn was bought in already prepared and then balled and ticketed with the Marriner label. The yarn was sold through a number of outlets but a good proportion went to Knitters World Ltd to be sold to their retail customers.

A small profit was made in 1984, but despite the efforts of the partners

Knitting pattern from Marriner Yarns Ltd.

the overall decline in hand knitting continued and in late October 1985 debts had accumulated and Marriner Yarns went into receivership. The Leeds firm of chartered accountants, Baker Rooke, appointed John Wilson and David Walker as joint receivers with much of the debt being owed to the firm's bank. Attempts were again made to sell the firm as a going concern. At that time the firm employed about twelve people with others employed by Fearn Publications which prepared the knitting patterns to go with the yarns.[10] As no purchaser for the firm was found the remaining assets were sold, the thirteen office and warehouse staff and seven sales personnel were made redundant. Marrriner Yarns Ltd was finally struck off the Companies Register in 1989.[11]

The Marriner logo as used today.

A small amount of stock and other assets was bought by Shaws (Cardiff) Ltd, who trade as Shaws the Drapers in South Wales and who also took over the Marriner name. For many years Shaws had bought yarn from Marriners, and their associate company Healey & Mathewman, who dealt with the non-branded trade. Shaws have an extensive chain of draper's shops in South Wales and wished to continue selling hand-knitting yarn with the Marriner name as it was well known and well liked by their customers. Shaws turned to another firm of spinners, Carter & Parker (Wendy Wools) Ltd of Guiseley near Leeds, for a supply of yarn. Carter & Parker now supply Shaws with all the popular hand-knitting types, such as four-ply, double knitting and Aran which are then wrapped with the Marriner label. This is still one of the leading brands of hand-knitting yarn in Wales and so, at the time of publication, it is still possible to buy Marriner's Yarns. The same well-established logo is used on the labels and also on the knitting leaflets.

## Conclusions

This study is a history of the firms that ran Greengate Mill or used the Marriner name for over two hundred years from 1784 to the present day. During that time the mill came under the control of many different partnerships and was the centre around which the activities of the early partnerships revolved. Many years later, the Marriner name was strong enough to be used for selling yarn after the mill had been destroyed and the last of the family had left the industry. Many changes were made both to the mill and to the way production was organised within the buildings. There were fundamental changes such as the substitution of worsted spinning for cotton and a large number of more gradual changes such as the development of new types of yarn. The firms running the mill may not have been typical of the West Riding textile industry but they were always typical of Keighley.

The development of the wool textile industry in the West Riding after 1750 can be seen as a continuous process. That development was not always uniform however, as changes in technology and trade played their part in speeding up or slowing down the industry's rise and eventual decline. Nevertheless, the connection between the development of the West Riding and its mills was not in doubt to publicisers of the area in 1893.

The mills have been the making of this part of Yorkshire, and their operations have conferred inestimable benefits upon countless thousands in every quarter of the globe, to whom a regular supply of useful and economical woollen fabrics has become a matter of the most vital importance.

The successful development of the wool textile industry in the West Riding, particularly in the area around Bradford and Halifax, has often obscured the fact that the cotton industry was also established there for a number of years. The power driven production of cotton yarn preceded the powered production of worsted yarn, and led to a geographical expansion of the cotton industry after 1780. Even in the area of the growing domestic worsted industry around Bradford and Halifax, sites were found for cotton mills, but nowhere was cotton stronger than in Keighley. Greengate Mill was a typical example of an early Keighley cotton mill and the first partnership to run the mill a typical example of local men putting money into a new enterprise. As with many other early Keighley firms only one of the partners had any experience of cotton spinning or running a mill. They were responding to a business opportunity created by the overall demand for cotton cloth which, for them, initially meant supplying the demands of the Lancashire hand loom weavers.

This early phase in the development of cotton spinning in Keighley shows how firms were prepared to overcome transport problems. Despite the distance from the merchants in Manchester and from the cotton weaving area around Blackburn, cotton spinning mills were established throughout the West Riding. From Sheffield to Sedbergh and Driffield to Bentham cotton mills ran successfully for many years. The early ledgers of Blakeys & Co. of Greengate Mill are rare in that they cover in detail the close links between a Yorkshire cotton spinning firm and its customers in Lancashire.

Following the introduction of cotton spinning mills into the West Riding came the development of cotton weaving. With an established domestic worsted weaving industry it was a logical step to put out cotton yarn to local weavers rather than send it to Lancashire. Cotton weaving was introduced in the Bradford area about 1800 and created additional work for the worsted weavers. As Keighley had the greatest concentration of cotton spinning mills in the area, cotton weaving became very important and Greengate Mill provided work for weavers over a large area.

When steam power became more readily available after 1800, and spinning machines were made with more and more spindles, the Yorkshire cotton mills started to look old fashioned. The earlier opposition to the new machines in Lancashire was halted and new and larger mills were built there, driving down prices. A new mill no longer need to be on a stream or river and could be larger to accommodate the new machinery. The partners at Greengate Mill followed the trend in Keighley and moved out of cotton spinning into worsted. The partnership also changed, with the Marriner family gaining complete control of the firm. The first William Marriner in Keighley was a draper, cotton spinner and manufacturer. His two sons, Benjamin and William had some experience of cotton, but quickly went into worsted manufacturing, and when they gained control of Greengate Mill, changed it over to worsted spinning.

From the establishment of worsted spinning at Greengate Mill in 1818, and until 1836, the firm of B & W Marriner operated as a typical West Riding worsted concern at the time. Wool was bought and then sorted and combed by hand. It was spun into yarn on the power driven frames in the mill and then given out to hand loom weavers to be made into cloth. The exception to this generally established pattern was that special types of yarn were spun by Marriners which were not used for cloth manufacture. Some cotton spinning may have been carried on until 1821, but from then on various types of special worsted yarns were produced which were not for their own consumption, or to be used by other local worsted manufacturers.

Although there is no evidence to show how many specialised weaving or spinning firms there were before 1850, the introduction of worsted power looms between 1833 and 1850 saw the combined spinning and weaving mill rise to a dominant position in the industry. The development of the worsted power loom and its general introduction into their mills by other manufacturers in the area coincided with Marriners giving up weaving. The reasons why Marriners concentrated on yarn production after 1835 are not recorded. The firm was well established and had employed hand loom weavers since 1814. The Marriner brothers apparently had adequate resources as they built a new spinning mill in 1837 and bought a steam engine for power. As part of their mill was let off to a worsted manufacturer they even had power looms on the premises. Their fellow manufacturers in Keighley started to use power looms at this time and one of them, John Brigg, was the brother-in-law of the two brothers. All the evidence would point to the Marriners having the resources to start power loom weaving yet the firm concentrated on spinning and in some ways was a forerunner of the specialist spinning firms which started to emerge after about 1856. Possibly the development by Marriners of specialist yarns for the carpet, braid, hosiery, hand-work and other markets had grown to such an extent by the early 1830s that power loom weaving did not seem to offer the same financial rewards.

Not enough is known about the relative quantities of the different types of yarn spun by Marriners during the nineteenth century to say which were the most important. Indeed it is not possible to say what percentage was sold at home, say through their agents, and what percentage was sold abroad. By the 1840s B & W Marriner were one of the many spinning firms selling yarn to the Bradford merchants. It is likely that a good proportion of their yarn was exported as the firms they sold to were very much concerned with the export trade. Later, as the practice in the continental yarn trade changed, Marriners sold through agents on the continent, especially in France. Their other significant market was the Midlands hosiery and knitting trade.

The expansion of the Greengate Mill premises during the 1860s and 1870s was a response to favourable trading conditions. Demand for worsted cloth rose at home and abroad with the specialist spinning firms being in a position to supply a wide range of yarns for the different markets.[12] The widespread use of cotton warps, which could now be used with a worsted weft, meant that weaving firms became used to buying in yarn from the specialist spinners. In addition, at this time Marriners were producing yarn for many different markets. They supplied the Midlands knitting industry, yarn for embroidery and fine hand work, carpet yarns, embroidery yarns, yarn for healds on looms, yarns for coat linings and many others. By diversifying Marriners were able to survive difficult periods and were in a position to switch production as demand fluctuated.

By 1880 Greengate Mill and the Marriner family were in a strong trading and financial position. They had invested in extensive new premises and were prepared for further expansion. The problem that they faced however, was the problem faced periodically by all family firms, that of inheritance. The death of one of the partners, which then required the payment of that partner's share to his or her executors, could distort the shareholdings of the surviving partners for generations. A more serious threat to the survival of a firm was a family or business dispute which resulted in the division of a firm. That was not infrequent in local textile firms. John Foster and his sons quarrelled about the partnership shares of Black Dyke Mills in 1865 and one of them thought that a break up of the partnership was imminent although it did not take place. A well known Keighley firm, James Haggas & Sons was split in 1852, when Damens Mill was split between James and William Haggas. Both brothers soon moved out to separate premises, as they needed space to expand their individual firms.

By 1888 three generations of the Marriner family had run the firm. The 'third generation' theme is a familiar one in West Riding folk lore. It usually meant that the material wealth acquired by the first two generations, often after many years of hard work, was missused by the grandsons, as their 'classical' education was followed by interests away from the mill. Life as a country gentleman was preferred to life as a mill owner and manager, with its necessary close attention to production and markets. The result was that the family had little interest in the firm apart from the wealth it provided and so the firm declined because of a lack of direct control. In the case of the Marriners that did not apply. Sons and daughters did go away to boarding schools but they were usually fairly local. Lister Marriner went to the Rev Paine's school in Dewsbury. One of his daughters went to Casterton, but a son went to the local grammar school in Keighley and another son, Raymond, served an apprenticeship.

The dissolution of the partnership between the Marriner brothers in 1888 and the division of Greengate Mill must have had a severe effect on the firm's profits. All their advisors were against the division but Lister Marriner and his brother Edward ignored all their pleas to reconsider their plan. It was Edward who argued most strongly for the firm to be divided, and in the end his brother had to agree. Like most of the early West Riding textile mills Greengate Mill had evolved with many additions when business was good. New buildings were added at all angles, as the need to accommodate more machinery grew year by year. Old buildings were relegated to more mundane uses such as warehousing but rarely dismantled. When lines were drawn, and buildings were allocated to the two brothers, it destroyed the unity of the mill with the two halves having far less value than the whole. Lister Marriner had made preparations by buying Hope Mill and, after twenty-four years, his son was able to buy back some of the buildings given to Edward. This meant that the Marriner name and firm could continue, but on a smaller scale than before. Most of the recently constructed buildings were lost for ever.

The year 1888 marks the end of the run of business records for the firm. Some letters and documents remain but there is no record of, say, production during the two World Wars or why the decision was made to concentrate on producing hand knitting yarns from the 1920s. Few personal papers of the Marriners survive with little detail about activities at the mill. When Raymond Marriner took over the firm in 1908 he would be unaware of the overall decline in the West Yorkshire worsted industry which would take place in his lifetime. He was twenty-six and had trained, not in textiles, but

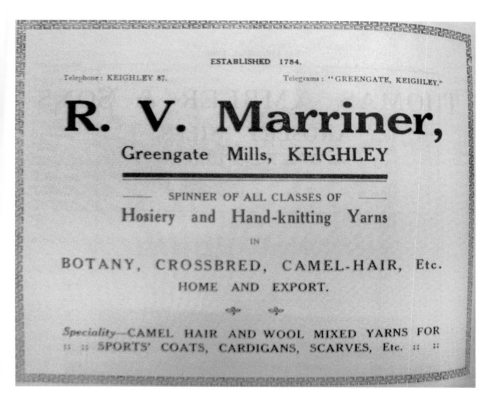

ESTABLISHED 1784.

Telephone: KEIGHLEY 87.          Telegrams: "GREENGATE, KEIGHLEY."

# R. V. Marriner,

## Greengate Mills, KEIGHLEY

—— SPINNER OF ALL CLASSES OF ——

### Hosiery and Hand-knitting Yarns

IN

## BOTANY, CROSSBRED, CAMEL-HAIR, Etc.

### HOME AND EXPORT.

*Speciality*—CAMEL HAIR AND WOOL MIXED YARNS FOR SPORTS' COATS, CARDIGANS, SCARVES, Etc.

as an electrical engineer. His brother Henry, who was nineteen years older, had been with the firm since before the argument between their father and uncle. However, he was one of the reasons for the argument, for Edward might not have insisted on the division, had Henry taken another job away from the mill. His unsuitability is shown by the recall of Raymond from his career with the Brush Electrical Company following the death of their father in 1906. The company immediately took his name, which was then retained for ninety years.

During the 1920s and 1930s Greengate Mill produced hand-knitting wool and a limited range of other yarns. Eventually Copleys of Manchester took the largest proportion of the output which was sold under their name. Following the Second World War the link with Copleys was broken and the decision was taken to sell knitting yarn through wool shops that existed in most towns. Hand knitting was a popular pastime in the 1950s and a way of producing a range of garments at a lower cost than machine knit. Wool was scarce and at times even old sweaters would be pulled back to be re-knit into new garments. Marriners established their own brand of knitting yarn and produced their own knitting leaflets. This was done by all the leading brands and there was strong competition to produce the most attractive designs, as the knitter would then buy the yarn recommended by the leaflet. Marriners played on the association of seamen with their name, as they had done in the past, and became one of the best known national brands.

Raymond Marriner's son John started in the firm in the 1930s and was the last of the Marriners to run the mill. His son, Benjamin, had a brief period as a model when he was a young boy in the 1940s but had no other connection with the firm. Hand knitting retained its popularity for some years after the Second World War with a number of brands, many based in West Yorkshire, competing for sales. However, Marriners did not have the capital or family interest to modernise and R V Marriner Ltd was sold to Union International in 1957. The Marriner name was kept as it was a strong brand in the knitting yarn market, but a general decline in interest in hand knitting started as machine knit garments became more fashionable and relatively cheaper. Following a disastrous fire in 1975 Greengate Mill was pulled down and Union International transferred staff to nearby Knowle Mill. Union International's experiment with textiles ended in 1983, but knitting yarn with the name Marriner on it could still be bought. It was more likely to be acrylic or nylon rather than wool, but the name was used to market knitting yarn by the firms that continued to own the brand.

It is perhaps fitting that the Marriner name should be the one thing that survives. The mill has gone, the family has gone from Keighley, but the name they established lives on. An attempt had been made to keep the Marriner Brass Band link with Keighley Town Band, but that went many years previously. Five generations of Marriners had been associated with textiles in Keighley. Now, there are just a few items in the local museum to illustrate the part they played in the development of the town; a link in the mayor's chain with Edward Marriner's name on it, the conductor's baton from

Marriners Brass band and a faded photograph of Raymond Marriner holding the cup the band won in 1909. An older generation of hand knitters still remember knitting with Marriner's Yarns and some still have the leaflets. Meanwhile, two hundred miles away in South Wales, hand-knitters can still buy Marrriner' yarns.

# CHAPTER SEVEN

# Marriner's Band

THE EARLY NINETEENTH CENTURY saw the formation of brass bands across the country, particularly in the north of England. Brass bands have been seen as a working class movement which flourished away from the large conurbations in the surrounding towns and villages where there was less entertainment than in the cities. Development of these bands was helped by the improvements made to the instruments which were commonly used at the time. Valves applied to the cornet and the later invention of the saxhorn family of instruments widened the range of instruments available and made for a more rounded sound. When the bands were formed the music they played was usually an arrangement of the classical works of the day, often opera or symphony related. Although bands were formed for many reasons, one argument for links with industrial firms was that they could be seen to decrease political activity by employees.

Many firms have supported brass bands that have borne their name. Employees usually formed the core of these bands that have had a number of uses, not least the promotion of the company name and the cementing of industrial relations. Marriner's Brass Band, as it eventually became, was founded by W L Marriner as a hobby, but the points mentioned were also relevant. Although the members in the early years had some say in the running of the band, soon its real position was, as Lister Marriner described it, his 'Private Brass Band'. He, and later his son, Raymond Marriner, spent a considerable amount of time organising and running the band.

Amongst the Marriner documents is a hard backed book with this hand written inscription on the title page ... The origin and progress of the Caminando Band; With a few short accounts of the most striking Incidents in connection with its formation. (Caminando is derived from the Spanish for walking or marching.)

There follows an account of the band from its establishment in 1845 until 1854. The first few paragraphs describe how it started.

This band was first commenced about the 12th of May 1844. It originated with Mr W L Mariner who, having heard some time previous the celebrated musicians Williams and his three sons perform on brass instruments in the Mechanics Institution, Keighley, felt a strong desire to form a band.

Having a bugle himself he assisted Holmes Emmott to procure a Tenor Trombone

and they practised together a short time. H E Got his instrument on the 20th May 1844 a few weeks afterwards W L M bought a Copper Cornopean at Bradford.

There is then a description of how other players obtained their instruments, how an instructor, George Gott, was found and how they practised in the engine house at the mill. The band formally came into existence on 12 January 1845 when the Rules and Regulations to be observed by the members of the Caminando Band were drawn up in a special book, which was also used for the band accounts. The reason for the rules was given ... As this brass band is formed for mutual amusement and instruction in music, and as peace and harmony are essential to its welfare, it is highly requisite that no dispute or angry feeling should arise among its members, therefore, for the prevention of any such occurrence, the following rules and regulations have been adopted.

The rules that followed dealt with such things as membership fees, choice of music, practice, absenteeism and voting. In all they had five members. The first public performance by these five was at the launching of a new boat on the mill dam on the 8 August 1845. The name Caminando was dropped after a short while.

During the following year membership rose and the musicians were asked to play at the Teachers' Tea Feast at the Church Sunday School on Easter Monday. They played during the tea, but their real test came later when they had to perform with the Keighley Choral Society in the evening. One member was so nervous that he paid someone to carry his instrument through the streets and had to fortify himself with whisky before the performance.

However, it appears to have been a success for the members decided that after this experience they ought to have a uniform. This, in the end, amounted to a blue cloth cap trimmed with gold, purchased from a local shop at a cost of 3s. od. each. In July 1846 they played at a supper to celebrate Lister Marriner's twenty-first birthday at which point he cleared the band's debt of £1 10s. 7d. (£1.53).

During the next few years the band played mainly for their own pleasure, but there were several engagements for which they were paid either in money or with a good meal. They were hired by the gentry of the town to entertain their guests at their houses and also to accompany visits to Bolton Abbey, a local beauty spot in Wharfedale. In November 1847 the rebuilding of the Parish Church was nearly complete and Lister Marriner obtained permission for the band to play on top of the tower, warmed by a cinder fire raised by a crane.[1]

In 1850 a full uniform was provided for the band members. They had blue frock coats, black trousers and caps most tastefully trimmed with gold lace. More engagements followed, for example playing every night for a month at an exhibition at the Mechanics' Institute. Lister Marriner then took the management of the band into his own hands. He paid the members for their shares in the stock of sheet music and supplied them with new instruments. For transport to their growing number of engagements he bought a horse drawn van. When he was married the employees of the firm were taken to Morecambe on a day trip, the band providing music for entertainment. This time, however, they travelled by train.

After Lister Marriner took over control of the band in 1852, the notes of general meetings and resolutions in the account book stopped as did the lists of subscriptions. Instead of being a joint effort between mill workers and mill owner the control shifted. This gave a more professional approach to running the band but gave the members less participation in its organisation. Lister Marriner dealt with the correspondence together with the decisions as to which engagements to accept. Once the fee for an engagement some distance away had been accepted he tried to obtain the lowest possible terms for rail transport if it was needed.

The *Keighley News* for 15 March 1913 carried an obituary for William Hainsworth Pickles who had died the previous Sunday aged 81. Mr Pickles went to work for Marriners in 1848 and joined the band the following year. He was an overlooker at Marrriners for 47 years was eventually asked to write an account of the band's activities. This was mainly a number of anecdotes about members of the band and the social and other activities at which they played. However, with the increasing professionalism of the band it relates also how it was decided that they should enter band contests. The first of these was at the Royal Gardens, Leeds, in 1855 when they won third prize. From this success the number of engagements increased and a number of concerts were organised by the band. The local story is that when the band met at the station to depart for this first competition, the crowd which had gathered doubted that they would win anything, shouting 'You'll win nowt', and calling them a 'bread and cheese

A concert programme featuring Marriner's Brass band.

band', from the suppers provided by Lister Marriner on the nights when they practised.[2]

In 1855 a series of band contests was started in the Zoological Gardens in Hull by Mr Enderby Jackson. He went on to organise many other contests in various parts of the country and eventually at the Crystal Palace, Sydenham, London. These major competitions ran for four years from 1860 and set the pattern for many more contests in other parts of the country with an increasing number of bands competing for the prize money. Enderby Jackson was the original driving force behind the contests which both raised standards and encouraged a good deal of local support for each band.

There was a strong local movement to form brass bands at this time and some members of Marriner's Band were tempted away to Harden Mill, near Bingley, to form a band there. Similarly the band was invited to play at Spring Head, the house of Hartley Merrall of Spring Head Mill, who was contemplating forming a band at Haworth. He must have gone ahead with this plan for in 1867 many members of Haworth Band were employees of the Merralls while one of the sons, George Merrall, was master of the band. As in Keighley there was a close link between this band and the local Volunteer corps for George Merrall was an ensign while the band played in military uniform at their parades.

During the 1850s Marriner's Band continued to play at shows and galas. Some of the personnel changed as trade was bad, and there was a movement away from the area. To maintain standards it was no longer possible to insist on all band members working at the mill. The constant practice and increased number of engagements led to the band entering more contests. A month after the third prize in 1855 at Leeds Royal Gardens they won a first prize there. In July 1860 the band was unsuccessful at the Crystal Palace in London, but in August of that year won the first prize at a brass band contest at Peel Park in Bradford. In 1861 Marriner's Band won a third prize on the 23 July at Crystal Palace and two days later a first prize together with a silver cup. The Saltaire Band won the main competition but Marriner's Band won The Sydenham Amateur Contest.

The *Daily Telegraph* had some interesting comments on the organisation of the first Crystal Palace competition and the competitors themselves:

The first 'Contest of Brass Bands' ever held in the south of England took place yesterday in the Crystal Palace. Unfamiliar as these contests are, even by name, to Londoners, such concours are held so continually in the northern districts that not a week passes during the summer months without the services of Mr Enderby Jackson, the zealous promoter of these scenes of friendly rivalry, being called in to requisition, to conduct and superintend a "contest' in some of the differing towns which by turns throw down the gauntlet of defiance to all comers. It was a happy thought of the inventor of the scheme to increase the proficiency of the executants and heighten interests in the most humanising and elevating of all pastimes, by fanning an esprit de corps, and sustaining it by the healthy excitement of emulation. It must be borne in mind that all the members of these bands, with the exception of the bandmaster, who in some cases, but by no means all, is a professional musician, are amateur performers, and have, moreover, invariably some daily occupation which absorbs nearly the whole of their time. The few hours in the week devoted to musical practice are therefore, of necessity very limited in number.

When Marriner's Band won the Sydenham Cup at Crystal Palace, one of the Keighley band members, John Midgley, who played a double B flat trombone of his own invention was awarded the first prize as the best bass player in the two day competition. In all thirty bands competed with the great majority of their members coming from what was described as the artisan class. The *Manchester Guardian* had some comments on the bass instruments of the five players which included John Midgley.

> This portion of the competition greatly excited the risible faculties of the assembly. The unwieldy instruments, the gruff and deep tones they emitted, the elephantine gambols they were made to execute, and the earnestness of the players, made the scene irresistibly comic.

It was felt that the general superiority of the Yorkshire bands was due to the better facilities they had for practice and the interest taken by the respective mill owners. An example of this was the Saltaire Band, which reputedly cost over £1000 a year to run besides the cost of entertaining the band members. Certainly Marriner's Band did not cost £1,000 a year, but they had their share of treats and tea drinking. Despite this they were usually more cheered by the bottles of gin slipped to them by Benjamin Marriner when he was present at any of their trips.

After their success in London more engagements followed, entailing a considerable amount of correspondence from Lister Marriner besides time given to practising and performing.[3] Eventually a junior band was formed by Joseph Turner to provide recruits for the senior band and this flourished for several years. Lister appeared to have complete control over who played in the band. For instance in June 1867 he wrote to Asa Waddington, one of the bandsmen ... As intimated to you a short time ago, Jonathon Preston has applied for his old place in the warehouse and in the Band and I have agreed to take him back. I am therefore under the necessity of asking you to forego your place in the Band for the present.

Similarly he wrote to a man called Calvert who was working at Hawick in Scotland, asking him to come back and play in the band. If he would agree to play in the band he would be given a job as a woolsorter with jobs found for his children. Lister Marriner said that he would pay him £1.os. od in this job, but that it was possible to earn £1 2s. od. (£1.10) to £1 3s. od. (£1.15) on piece rates. The only trouble was that houses were hard to find in Keighley, but Calvert could have a cottage in the mill yard for a few days until he found a house for himself and his family. Calvert must have been a good bandsman for Lister sent him £4 to help with the cost of moving back to Keighley.

Managing the activities of the band at the height of their success must have taken a fair part of Lister Marriner's time judging by the letters he was sending to people who wanted the band to play at their gala or special occasion.

I am instructed by the members of my Band to say that they will be very glad to join the Bacup Band in giving a concert on Saturday week the 9th inst. They are at a loss what amt. to state as an engagement, not knowing what the expenses will be. I however think they ought to have £15 but if this is more than you can honestly give will you please reply by return what is the most you can say and what the expenses are likely to be. What did you give Black Dyke last year? 27 September 1865

Another letter in reply to someone who wanted Marriner's Band to play at a tea feast in July 1868 explained that ... Today they are going to Bradford to play for the Band of Hope children at their Gala in Peel Park. They will muster about 2,000 and will sing several pieces, the band accompanying them.

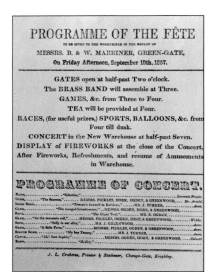

Programme for a Fete and Concert, 1857.

Marriner's Band achieved national honours besides having a very high reputation locally. Prizes were won at competitions in Birmingham Ripon, Stalybridge, Lancaster, Skipton and Nelson. They provided music for countless Sunday School treats and Agricultural Society shows, they played military music for the Volunteers and classical music at formal concerts. Blue uniforms were worn for most engagements but the band wore grey uniforms when they played as the band of the 35th West Yorkshire Volunteers.

The national competitions were revived in 1900 by John Henry Iles who organised a new series of national events at Crystal Palace and also at Belle Vue in Manchester. He was another business man who understood that it was necessary to encourage local support for each band and who was

Marriner's Band 1909. R V Marriner with the cup.

able to mobilise publicity for these contests. An unused Thousand Guinea Trophy was found in the Crystal Palace vaults and became the focus for the contests. Support was obtained from the leading bands and the British National Championships for brass bands have continued, apart from the war years, until the present day.

Marriner's Band had a revival before the First Word War when it again won a cup at Crystal Palace in 1909, although not the main prize. This was one of the preliminary cups and was awarded by the Daily Mirrror. Raymond Marriner had followed his father with his interest in music and became bandmaster until the band was merged with Keighley Town Band in 1912.[4] A link was retained however, for the bandsmen of Keighley Town Band had the initial M on their caps. In the 1930s the band still rehearsed in the band room at Greengate Mill where some of the old uniforms were kept.

**Marriner**

# CHAPTER EIGHT

# *Mill memories*

I N J A N U A R Y 2003 the author had a feature in the *Keighley News* asking former employees to provide him with their memories of working for Marriners. Some remarkable stories emerged which provided insight into working conditions in the mill and provided previously unknown information about the continued use of the Marriner name in the sale of knitting yarn. Memories spanned a period of about fifty years and touched on both the technical aspects of preparing yarn for sale and of everyday working in the mill. The technical aspects have been incorporated into Chapter 6, as have the details about the use of the Marriner brand name. However, the stories of the people who worked at the mill, or who had some connection with the Marriner family are given here, sometimes just as they provided them.

**Mrs Doris Moore** remembers her grandfather James Chamberlain working at Greengate Mill for fifty years between 1898 and 1948. During that time he didn't have a day of work for illness and hardly ever took any holiday. The reason for that was that he was the mill engineer and when the mill, like all

Workers at Greengate Mill about 1920. Raymond Marriner at the table.

Weathervane at Greengate Mill. A sailor leaning on a capstan and looking through a telescope. Or the old man checking to see if you were working!

the others in Keighley, closed for Keighley Feast Week he was busy with maintenance work on the engine and shafting. Until electric motors were installed in the mill he was responsible for the steam engine which drove all the machinery. He also worked long hours as he was responsible for sounding the 'buzzer' to call people to work in a morning. Jim Chamberlain was a big man which was useful when he had heavy metal parts to move. Doris can remember seeing him around the mill and also in the engine room which like all engine rooms was kept spotlessly clean. You had to wipe your feet before you went in and all the brightwork on the engine was highly polished. When Jim had a quiet period he would sit in an old arm chair in the engine room just listening to the engine and he could hear the slightest change in rhythm which needed attention with the oil-can. He had originally trained as a millwright at the BDA (Bradford Dyers Association) but moved to Marriners when he was 22 years old. Even after he retired at the age of 72 he still returned to the mill to see his old friends. Doris's father followed in Jim's footsteps and became the boiler firer at Greengate Mill but later left to become an engineer for another firm.

Doris remembers that the main product of the mill was knitting yarn and during the 1930s a popular type was called Lady Bettie which Marriners had produced for many years. She also has good memories of Ray Mariner and his son John. They gave the local scout troop use of the mill van to take their tents to the summer camp site and their house, Shann Manor, was always available for the Parish Church summer garden party.

**Mrs Lord** brought my attention to a book about Patrick Bronte which was co-authored by her late husband.[1] In this book are details of a letter from Patrick Bronte to Benjamin Marriner dated 10 November 1824. In the letter the Rev Bronte is requesting the withdrawal of money from the Savings Bank to pay for his daughter Emily to go away to school.

Mrs Lord also tells the story of going to Greengate Mill when she was a young girl during the Second World War. They went to collect knitting wool in khaki, navy blue and air force blue shades and were allowed to fetch this from skeps in the mill. When they returned home she, together with family and friends, knit the wool into socks and scarves, but being young, she had to have help from her aunt to turn the heel on the socks. These were later packed into boxes by her mother before being sent away.

**Mrs Hilda Lyness** followed her mother and grandmother into the textile trade. Her grandmother worked at the flax spinning mill at Clifford near Boston Spa before moving to Keighley. Her mother started working for Marriners at Greengate Mill in 1908 at the age of 12 and worked weeks of alternate mornings and afternoons with school taking up the other part of the day. She had a wage of 4s. 6d. (22p) per fortnight and had to hand this over to her parents. She retired from the mill about 1956 having worked there all her life. Hilda started work in the spinning department at Marriners in 1937, but left in 1940 to work in a munitions factory and went into office work after the war. However, despite only working for the firm for a few years she has happy memories of those days. She relates how in 1938 Marriners were the first firm in Keighley to pay their workers holiday pay for the annual holiday of Keighley Feast and she received 22s. 6d. (£1.12). When this extra wage was given out Raymond Marriner and his son John were cheered and clapped by the mill workers. Hilda was able to lend me two photographs taken at the mill. The first shows a group of ladies standing in front of a Prince Smith & Stells spinning frame dated 1931 with her mother standing at the back on the right. However, the space above the machines is highly decorated with bunting, flags and balloons. Some of the ladies are also wearing novelty hats for this was the celebration for the jubilee of King George V in

Ladies in spinning section celebrating King George V's Jubilee 1935.

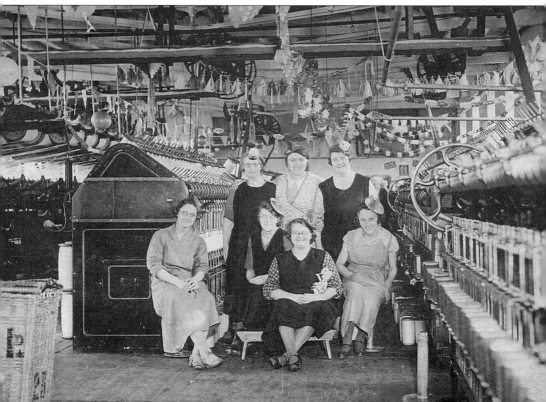

Staff outside Greengate Mills before trip to Blackpool to celebrate John Marriner's 21st birthday. Raymond and John Marriner are on the left.

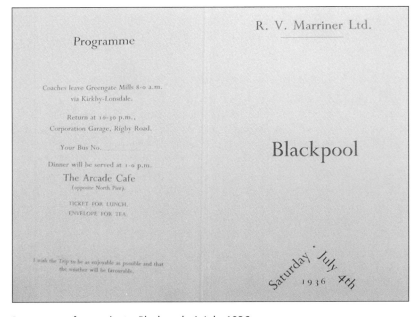

Programme for a trip to Blackpool, 4 July 1936.

1935. Another photograph shows the entire workforce waiting outside the mill to set of to Blackpool to celebrate the 21st birthday of John Marriner. Raymond Marriner is on the left with John next to him and then the mill manager. Somewhere in the crowd is Hilda's mother. Some of the girls with sailors' hats look as though they really intend to enjoy themselves when they arrive in Blackpool.

Hilda remembered the private footbridge over the river Worth which had been build many years before to enable William Marriner to cross over from his house at Worthville. She also remembered the Co-op bakery shop near the mill where workers bought pies, pasties and cakes and the wool shop which Marriners ran in Church Green. A recent visit to the site of the mill had distressed her with derelict buildings replacing the smart mill premises and well kept terrace houses of nearly seventy years ago.

One lady wrote to tell her story – *I left school Christmas 1952, 15 years old and went straight to Marriners. My mum helped me get a job there. First wage 7/6d [37p] for week. Mum gave me ½ crown [13p] to make it up to 10/– [50p]. First job learning how to do shade cards for customers, for selection of colours etc. I went through inspecting wool (for defects), hanking, winding wool on to cones, balling wool from the cones and spinning, twisting, packing. So if we were called to help out elsewhere we would know what to do. Old Mr Ray Marriner would come round watching us work and have a word. Then John Marriner followed on. Good people to work for. Worked from 7.30–5.30. 1 hour lunch. 10 minute break morning/ afternoon. Used to be the Co-op bakery across road. Nipped out to get cakes for lunches and pasties. Mr Ray Marriner had his own number plate on car – RVM 1. My mum looked after Marriners shop in Church Green for a few years. I enjoyed my years working there and even went back for evening work after getting married and having a family.*

**Henry Calvert**, from Cross Hills between Keighley and Skipton, had no connection with Marriners but has a story which says something about the value townspeople put on Raymond Marriner. During the Second World War, when Henry was serving in Italy, his father was very ill and dying. His mother was distraught and wanted her son Henry to have some leave to be able to return to Keighley and help. Although she didn't work for him the person she turned to was Raymond Marriner. He was sympathetic, but unable to assist, and Henry's father died whilst he was in Italy. However, Henry has remembered this and told me the story to illustrate the standing of Raymond Marrriner in the town.

**Martha Scott** wrote to say that: *my maiden aunt worked as a reeler at R V Marriners and I and my siblings all worked there when we left school at 14 years. I became a spinner in 1942, we clocked on at 7.00 a.m. and off at 5.00 p.m. We had a one hour lunch break.*

*I slept in one day on the first week (rising at six o'clock in the morning was hard). Ten shillings was docked from my pay which made a spinners wage £2 10s. od.*

*a week. Our family was poor before the war started, we got poorer and the rich richer. I don't suppose your book will be about slave labour.*

*The only good thing about Marriners happened in 1948. I was married at St Anne's Church, but because ours was a mixed marriage we were not allowed flowers on the altar. Fortunately, someone from the Marriner family was also marrying that morning before us. The altar and church was over filled with flowers. Poetic justice or what?*

*I have a knitted garment with the Marriner label which was used as a demonstration model in the mill shop.*

*New mill hands had to be initiated with a ride round the mill yard. The doffer lads bundled me into a skip and pushed me round the cobbled yard, it was a bumpy ride. I told my Nan what a terrible place I thought Marriners was. She said, 'Never mind Puttie, at least you have a job'.*

**Lilian Hyde** worked at the mill from 1943 to 1946 and gave me four knitting leaflets, three from the period after the 1975 fire when Marriners operated from Knowle Mill and one from Marriner Yarns of Pitt Street in Keighley. Although she was a young girl at the time Lilian has happy memories of working at Marriners and remembered Raymond Marriner walking round the mill in a morning to keep an eye on what was going on. The overlooker in the fly-spinning section where she worked was Harry Watson and the mill manager at the time was Mr Thomas. Production at the time was geared towards the war effort with much of the yarn being in colours suitable for the armed services.

**Gordon Buchanan** worked at the mill from 1964 to 1969 as an apprentice overlooker in the drawing department. As an apprentice overlooker he attended Keighley Technical College for training. The college had a textile department at the time although it was soon closed and the staff transferred to Bradford Technical College.

The machinery used during his time in Greengate Mill was a mixture of very old, old and fairly new. The series of machines they had for producing yarn was the old 'Bradford System' plus the newer 'Raper Autoleveler' system. They had some old machines made by Hall & Stell as well as some old fly spinning frames converted to spin mohair. The old machinery was very reliable as there was little to go wrong with it. Fancy yarns were spun including some with a metallic element and during the time when he was there they opened a gilling section in order to be able to spin lovats.

Long fibre wool was used to make knitting yarn. This meant heavy machinery, usually fly spinning. They made fleck yarn with mohair which was scoured after spinning and also made 4 fold yarn. Hanking machines were used in the mill as hanks were cheaper to make than balls.

There was no combing done at the mill so tops were bought in from Bulmer & Lumb and Sir James Hill in Bradford or from Low Mill in Keighley which was run by J P Heaton, part of the same group. He felt that part of the reason for the eventual decline of the firm was the lack of investment in new machinery.

Over 100 people worked at the mill at that time. The mill manager was Jack Yeadon and the General Manager was a Mr Dunn.

Gordon told me two stories from his time as a young man at Greengate Mill. One day he was instructed to burn all the rubbish that had accumulated in the section where he worked. He swept round the machines and collected everything to put into the firm's new incinerator which he carefully stacked. Unfortunately he had put in a lot of plastic which burnt fiercely. When he looked out of the window the incinerator was glowing red, then white and finally disintegrated into twisted metal. His second story comes from a year or two later when, on the night shift, he met the manager making a surprise visit. Several of his friends were having a quick drink in the nearby pub so he ran round to tell them to get back to work. The landlord was surprised to see that Gordon stayed on for a drink but, as he said, 'No need to hurry back, he's already seen me at work.'

One very useful piece of information Gordon provided was that the Marriner name was linked with the firm of Carter & Parker (Wendy Wools) Ltd from the late 1980s.

**Margaret Pethers** sent a cutting from the *Keighley News* of 4 March 1950 which was part of the paper's Local Industries Series at the time. The cutting was about Marriners and was headed 'A Textile Business of Five Generations'. As well as giving a short history of the firm the cutting included photographs of people who worked for the Marriners at the time. These included herself as Miss Peggy McKniff who had a job ticketing hanks before she was married.

**Pip Hayes** worked as an accountant for the Union International Company (Vesteys) when they bought J P Heaton Ltd who ran Low Mill in Keighley. Other local textile firms were bought which would enable South American wool from Vestey's meat business to be processed right through to a final product which was to be knitting wool. These firms were Healey & Mathewman of Bradford as well as Marriners, while a new company was set up to buy and sort wool. This was J W Allen Ltd. The firm of R V Marriner was absorbed into J P Heaton from the point of view of senior management and production. Pip remembered Ray Marriner, who was seventy-seven, when they sold out to Vesteys in 1957. He also remembered his son John who stayed on for about six years after and acted as general manager at Greengate Mill. At the time Marriners had a sales force of about twenty representatives who were based around the country but had their annual sales conference in Yorkshire at Craiglands Hotel in Ilkley.

**Allan Greenwood** worked for Marriners as did his brother Stanley. Alan always wanted to be a joiner but couldn't find a job in that trade so he worked in the mill from 1947 to 1950 and then again after National Service until 1954 when he left to go to Grove Mill. He regarded Ray Marriner as 'a real gentleman' and recalled how he would come round the mill about 9.00 o'clock in the evening just before the end of the evening shift. He often wore a fawn suit with highly polished brown brogues and left a faint smell of whisky behind him. Ray Marriner was obviously anxious that the quality of yarn produced was as high as possible. He had a habit of checking the empty bobbins on the spinning frames for fluff and dirt as he walked round. This could be caught up in the yarn as it was wound onto the bobbins so he would inspect the bobbins and pull off any fluff he found. Allan quickly found that if his spinners ensured the bobbins were clean, Mr Ray would not bother them too much and they could finish their shift on time. Alan found two photographs with one taken in the mill when it was trimmed up for Queen Elizabeth II's coronation and an older one showing a Ray Marriner and a group of workers in the 1920s.

**Ron Barritt** later became a very successful physiotherapist and toured abroad several times when he was physiotherapist to the British Lions Rugby League team. However, he started at Greengate Mill as a young boy during World War II. His first job was to find and bring back spare bobbins and recollects being in great trouble if he didn't bring back enough to satisfy his overlooker. After serving in the Royal Signals he returned to Marriners as an overlooker until about 1953 when he moved to another textile firm. As an overlooker he has been able to help with technical details about production and the machinery used in the mill at the time.

Ron lived very near to the mill, as did his aunt who worked for him later. Like Alan Greenwood above, he remembered the evening shifts and the long hours during the war, particularly for those who had to stay overnight for fire watch duties. After the war many of the people at the mill joined the union but one incident, when the union secretary appeared to be taking the side of the management prompted Ron to resign despite the fact that a wage increase was imminent. He had to negotiate his own increase with Ray Marriner but finished up getting slightly more than the others. Ray Marriner and his son John were strong supporters of the Conservative Party. Ray asked Ron if he would like to go to a Conservative event at Swindon Castle near Masham and take some friends if he wished. He chose two staunch Labour party members, for, as he said to Ray Marriner, it was no good taking anyone who already was a conservative. Unfortunately they had a few drinks before the event and, as they were late, had to sit at the front. One of them fell asleep, started to snore and they were all ordered to the back.

**Annie Lund** was someone else who started with Marrriners but went on to success in a completely different career, this time as the deputy-head of a school. Annie started at the mill aged 15 in 1932 and worked there until the start of the war. Despite failing eyesight Annie supplied pages of notes on her memories from the 1930s. These are some of them. Mr Ray, as he was called, was a sidesman at Keighley Parish Church and a man of strong principles. The mill was always closed on Good Friday and Easter Monday but if they were busy, people had to work on the Saturday morning. A number of disabled people were employed at the mill and Ray was chairman of the local hospital board. All employees were expected to pay 1d per week to the hospital fund. At that time there was an annual hospital ball and employees were given free tickets which Raymond paid for. However, money for the supper was only given out when people were actually on the premises.

One feature of the time, which would be unpopular now, was the sounding of a buzzer to alert workers to the time left to be at work. This went at 5.40 p.m., 6.00 a.m. and 1.30 p.m. If anyone turned up, even a few seconds late after the buzzer stopped at 6.00 a.m. they lost two and a half hours pay.

Annie can remember the layout of the mill with the offices and production facilities finishing with ticketing. Although no yarn was normally sold with a Marriner label some was sold with other names such as Rosedale Wool. White and baby wool was prepared in a special way that took some time to learn. Embroidery wool was also spun and the hanks of this wool were packed in boxes of twelve. Although Marriners sold through wholesalers at this time, they did sell some of their hand-knitting wool to employees and local people. Initially this was done from a small one-roomed building but later it was sold from a shop on the corner of South Street and Greengate Road. Later still it was sold with a Marriner ticket from a shop on Church Green.

When times were slack Annie helped with cone winding and what was known as tin-hat winding. At the time she was learning shorthand and at lunchtime would take some spare paper from packs of stoved wool and practice her shorthand outlines. Mr Raymond found her doing this, which impressed him, but it then meant that if anyone in the office was away, Annie was asked to help out. In those days office work started at 9.00 a.m. so Annie had to work in the mill from 6 o'clock for three hours before transferring to the office. One job was to prepare shade cards and she remembers two colours that were listed as Marina and Margaret-Rose. Sydney Marriner, who was Ray's twin brother, wanted Annie to be his secretary but Ray refused. The reason he gave was that there were plenty of secretaries but Annie couldn't be replaced in the balling department. However, Mr Sydney gave her a carved wooden plaque from his office which she still has. Annie's wage throughout this time was 23s. 0d. less 1s. 9d. deductions. Annie's final memory of Greengate Mill is the fire in October 1975 which she happened to see and prompted her account which is added below.

**Edna Simpson** worked in the despatch department and then in the leaflet section from about 1955 to 1962. Marriners had a number of sales representatives who were based in different parts of the country and called on the retailers. To help with sales, fashion shows were held in various parts of the country for the retailers and Edna was involved with their organisation.

Knitting leaflets always specified the required tension but many knitters ignored these details and complained if the garment finished up too small or too large. A small laundry was built, mainly to wash display garments. On one ocassion a child's garment was returned with the complaint that 'it had washed stiff'. Ten attempts in the laundry failed to remove all the soap.

**Ann Wade** worked at Marriners for twenty-five years, firstly for R V Marriner Ltd and then for Marriner Yarns Ltd, until she was made redundant in

1985. Ann's twenty-five years therefore spanned the time from when Ray Marriner still came to the mill, until the end of Marriners in Keighley. She worked in one of the offices doing a variety of jobs but mainly concerned with the orders for yarn. These came in from the reps, by letter and by telephone. As the cost to the retailer of holding stocks grew, orders became smaller and would often just be for a few pounds of yarn. Later orders were in kilograms and grams, as knitting yarn had to be retailed in these weights. Ann has good memories of the early years working at Greengate Mill. There was a happy atmosphere in the mill and staff were not made to feel uncomfortable if they needed to visit the doctor or dentist in working hours.

Ann was at work when the fire started in October 1975. The office seemed to be getting very warm and then smoke started coming through the floorboards. Although the alarm was raised they were asked to go back inside several times to collect files and typewriters. After the fire some of the staff, including Ann, were moved to Hope Mill which had been used for storage. From Hope Mill Ann moved to Knowle Mill where the company rented several floors and there was plenty of space.

With the decline in hand knitting Union International decided to sell their Keighley textile interests and the stock of Marriner's yarn was sold to Edward Arnold and Robert Feather who set up Marriner Yarns Ltd. Ann then moved to their premises at Pitt Street for two years before the firm went into liquidation.

Annie Lund, who gives her story above about when she worked at Greengate Mill in the 1930s, saw the fire in 1975 and wrote this story.

## The old mill on fire

The old mill was on fire and the spectators who had rushed to the scene saw smoke.

I too saw smoke, but much more. I saw 'Pictures in the fire'.

Whereas others could only smell the stench of burning wool,I could also small the oil as it rose from the floorboards and filled my nostrils, as I entered, for the first time, the door which was crackling in the fire.

Once again I saw two elderly sisters, with their home-knitted green shawls hanging loosly round their heads, the ends dangling over their black smocks, and on their feet, brass-framed clogs that clattered across the stone flags in the cellar.

I recall being terrified when I saw the two hooks hanging over fifty feet in space in the hoist, when I realised that the jobber-boy was hanging the skip, with me inside, on to them. As I fell through space, I could see the dim light through the cracks of the wicker-basket. The look of surprise on the face of one of the sisters when she found a girl inside the skip, instead of yarn, was amazing. In 1935, as we celebrated the Silver Jubilee amidst the machinery and wool, a cardboard-framed picture of King George V and Queen Mary hung between long red, white and blue paper curtains, and Union Flags decorated the walls.

No-one as surprised to see the look of horror on the mill-owner's face when, one Christmas, he was grabbed and kissed under the mistletoe by one of the young mill-lasses. However, all were delighted to see the box of oranges which he sent to repay her.

It was a very dusty room, where the mill band had practised for well over fifty years. Piles of spent matches were scattered around the floor. To one side of the door was an old oak chest. I opened it and took out the old band uniforms, one at a time. Obviously from the different styles, they had belonged to three generations of musicians. At the bottom of the chest I found an old battered trumpet, the silver of which had long gone black, won as a prize by the band many years before.

It was 11.00 a.m. on 11 November. The shrill whistle of the buzzer let the whole area know that it was a time to remember. The engines slowed down. The machinery stopped. All was still. No sound outside either. The young jobber-boy dropped to his knees and bowed his head. We joined him in the same attitude, remembering those who had sacrificed all, pledging to God that we would try to make a better world.

The old mill is now demolished. A new road is being built in its place, but whenever I pass that way I will always see 'Pictures in the fire'.

Annie Lund kindly gave me permission to include both her poem 'Mills' and 'The Old Mill on Fire' which were published by Arnold-Wheeton in 1982 in *Wheels. An Industrial Anthology*. This was a publication designed to promote work in industry and was part of an initiative called 'Understanding British Industry', which was sponsored by the CBI

# Some textile and other terms used in the text

| | |
|---|---|
| Amens | cloth woven with a pattern |
| Andalusian | fine worsted material made from Spanish merino wool |
| Berlin Wool | single or ply good quality worsted yarn used for embroidery |
| Bombazines | cloth with a silk warp. |
| Callimancoes | cloth used for ladies' petticoats and chair seating |
| Carding | a treatment before spinning to open and mix the fibres |
| Combing | separating process for long wool. The long fibres (tops) are spun into worsted yarn |
| Camlets | cloth used for making cloaks, but most were exported to China and the East Indies |
| Doffer | person who replaces full bobbins with empty ones on a spinning frame |
| Drawboys | cloth with a woven pattern which originally required the help of a boy with the weaving |
| Drawing | a process where the loose rope of fibres is drawn out before spinning |
| Fleecy | a soft yarn used for coat linings |
| Floss | used for embroidery |
| Genappe yarn | the yarn is heated or singed to remove loose fibres. Used for braids and trimmings |
| Heald yarn | hard yarn used for healds through which the warp threads pass in a loom |
| Knitting yarn | this has a low twist and should be uniform, flexible and smooth |
| Ladybettie | yarn for a popular cloth in the late nineteenth century produced for lady's dresses |
| Lastings | a thick fabric only 18 inches wide |
| Moreens | cloth used for bed curtains and furniture |
| Noils | the short fibres from worsted combing which are used for woollen cloth |
| Overlooker | foreman in a mill |
| Roving | the name usually given to the prepared fibres ready for drawing |
| Russels | cloth used for ladies' petticoats, boots, shoes and men's waistcoats |

| | |
|---|---|
| Says | a cloth, heavier than a shalloon and exported to Spain and Italy to make priests' robes |
| Sets | small paving stones or cobles |
| Shetland | used for hosiery and knitting |
| Shalloons | a cloth used for women's dresses. A great number were dyed scarlet and exported to Turkey |
| Stuffs | an old name for worsted cloth |
| Tammies | cloth used for ladies' dresses with large numbers being exported. |
| Tops | the long wool fibres produced during worsted combing |
| Wildbores | cloth like a Tammie but made from lower quality wool |
| Worsted | a smooth cloth made from combed wool |

# Notes

## Notes to Chapter 1

1. E. M. Sigsworth, *Black Dyke Mills* (1958), p. 11.
2. J. Hodgson, *Textile Manufacture in Keighley* (1879), Reprinted 1999. p. 16.
3. Hodgson, op.cit., p. 90.
4. Hodgson, op.cit., pp. 176–9.
5. *Halifax Journal* 16 Feb. 1805.
6. Sigsworth, op.cit., p. 20.
7. E. M. Sigsworth, 'The West Riding Wool Textile Industry' *Wool Knowledge*, Spring 1952, p. 16.
8. E. M. Sigsworth, 'William Greenwood and Robert Heaton', *Bradford Textile Society Journal* (1951/2), pp. 61–72.
9. Hodgson, op.cit., pp. 47–8.
10. Hodgson, op.cit., p. 65.
11. Hodgson, op.cit., p. 82.
12. Hodgson, op.cit., pp. 212–13.
13. G. A. Miller, *Blackburn, The Evolution of a Cotton Town* (1951), p. 330.
14. See G. Ingle, *Yorkshire Cotton* (1997), for details of the early Yorkshire cotton industry.

## Notes to Chapter 2

1. Hodgson, op.cit., p. 52.
2. Marriner Papers, Box 96, LUL.
3. Marriner Papers, Box 96, LUL.
4. Marriner Papers, Box 107, LUL.
5. *Leeds Mercury*, 19 July 1785.
6. *Leeds Intelligencer*, 5 May 1789
7. G. W. Daniels, *The Early English Cotton Industry* (1920), p. 69.
8. Hodgson, op.cit., p. 53.
9. Marriner Papers, Box 82, LUL.
10. S. Dumbell, Early Liverpool Cotton Imports and the Organisation of the Cotton Market in the Eighteenth Century, *Economic Journal, vol. Xxxiii* (1923), pp. 362–73.

11. M. M. Edwards, *The Growth of the British Cotton Trade* (1967), p. 10.

12. G. Unwin, *Samuel Oldknow and the Arkwrights* (1924), p. 100.

13. Edwards, op.cit., p. 227.

14. G. A. Miller, *Blackburn, The Evolution of a Cotton Town* (1951) p. 393.

15. *Leeds Mercury*, 21 September 1784.

16. G. Unwin, *Samuel Oldknow and the Arkwrights* (1924), p. 100.

17. Miller, op.cit., p. 393.

18. *Leeds Intelligencer*, 16 December 1799.

## Notes to Chapter 3

1. G. W. Daniels, *The Early English Cotton Industry* (1920), p. 132.

2. W. Cudworth, *Rambles Round Horton* (1886), p. 30.

3. G. H. Brown, *On Foot Round Settle* (1896), p. 143.

4. Hodgson, op.cit., pp. 227–8.

5. Hodgson, op.cit., p. 230.

6. Marriner Papers, Box 77.

7. *Leeds Intelligencer*, 10 April 1787.

8. Returns made to the Clerk of the Peace under Statutes GEO III, 1802. An Act for the preservation of the health and morals of apprentices and others employed in cotton and other mills. WYAS. Wakefield.

9. *Halifax Journal*, 12 February 1803.

10. This section is based on work carried out by Dr Gillian Cookson on Keighley textile machinery makers and I am grateful for her help.

11. Marriner Papers, Box 21.

12. *The Commercial Directory for 1814–15* (Manchester).

## Notes to Chapter 4

1. *Leeds Intelligencer*, 21 August 1797.

2. G. Unwin, *Samuel Oldknow and the Arkwrights* (1924), p. 4.

3. Marriner Papers, Box 50.

4. Hodgson, op.cit., p. 54.

5. J. James, *History of the Worsted Manufacture in England* (1857), p. 401.

6. James, op.cit., p. 405.

7. J. Hodgson, op.cit., p. 141.

8. *Leeds Mercury*, 13 May 1826.

9. Hodgson, op.cit., p. 143.

10. Hodgson, op.cit., p. 161.

11. Hodgson, op.cit., p. 160.

12. E. M. Sigsworth, The End of Hand Loom Weaving, *Bradford Textile Society Journal* (1957/8). pp. 69–72.

13. James, op.cit., p. 414.

14. *Leeds Mercury*, 22 July 1826.

15. Hodgson, op.cit., p. 241.
16. James, op.cit., p. 383.
17. Marriner Papers, Box 64.
18. D. T. Jenkins, *The West Riding Wool Textile Industry 1770–1835*, p. 169.
19. Marriner Papers, Box 95.
20. Marriner Papers, Box 95.
21. *Bradford & Huddersfield Courier*, 18 May 1826.
22. Marriner Papers, Box 95.
23. Hodgson, op.cit., p. 153.
24. Hodgson, op.cit., p. 48.
25. Marriner Papers, Box 86. LUL.
26. Hodgson, op.cit., p. 195.
27. Hodgson, op.cit., p. 54.
28. Hodgson, op.cit., p. 54.
29. Hodgson, op.cit., p. 54.
30. Hodgson, op.cit., p. 139.
31. *Leeds Mercury*, 2 August 1834.
32. E. E. Dodd, The Bradford Strike of 1825, *Bradford Textile Society Journal* (1966/67), pp. 100–4.
33. Reports from the Commissioners appointed to collect information in the Manufacturing Districts, relative to Employment of Children in Factories, and as to the propriety and means of curtailing the hours of their labour
    First Report BPP. (1833) (450) XX
    Second Report BPP. (1833) (519) XXI.
    Supplementary Reports, BPP. (1834) (167) XIX, XX.
34. W. Keighley, *Keighley, Past and Present*, (1879), p. 119.
35. J. Lock and Canon W. T. Dixon, *A Man of Sorrow. The Life and Times of the Rev. Patrick Bronte. 1771–1861* (1979) p. 255.

## Notes to Chapter 5

1. Marriner Papers, Box 95.
2. Marriner Papers, Box 95.
3. Marriner Papers, Box 70.
4. Marriner Papers, Box 107.
5. Marriner Papers, Box 95.
6. B & W Marriner to Benjamin Bedford, Hope Mill, Keighley, 10 November 1874.
7. See Chapter 3.
8. E. M. Sigsworth, *Black Dyke Mills* (1958), p. 65.
9. Sigsworth, op.cit., p. 222.
10. F. A. Wells, *The British Hosiery and Knitwear Industry* (1972). p. 118.
11. Ibid, p. 131.
12. Ibid, p. 122.
13. B & W Marriner to Herman Stercken, Berlin. 23 March, 1874.

14. B & W Marriner to Bechenbach & Co., Bradford. 5 December, 1873.
15. *The Century's Progress* (1893). p. 203.
16. Marriner Papers, Box 56.
17. James, op.cit., p. 506.
18. James, op.cit., p. 508.
19. Marriner Papers, Box 107.
20. A. Briggs, Industry and Politics in Early Nineteenth Century Keighley, *The Journal of the Bradford Historical and Antiquarian Society, Vol. II. New Series.* pp. 305–17.
21. Briggs, op.cit., p. 306.
22. Hodgson, op.cit., p. 95.
23. Editorial, *The Woollen, Worsted and Cotton Journal, Vol I,* November 1853.
24. James, op.cit., p. 548.
25. Hodgson, op.cit., p. 55.
26. H. A. N. Hallam, The Listers of Frizinghall, *The Bradford Antiquary, New Series, Part XLIV.* 1969.
27. Marriner MS., Box 70.
28. Marriner MS., Box 86.
29. Marriner MS., Box 96.
30. William Naylor and Ellis Myers had taken over the job of Spencer Booth who was mentioned in the first list of duties. William Naylor eventually became manager and later a partner with Lister Marriner.
31. Marriner Papers, Box 96.
32. Marriner Papers, Box 56.
33. Marriner Papers, Box 52. Isaac Booth was the architect for B & W Marriner.
34. Isaac Booth to Lister Marriner, 21 October 1876.
35. Marriner Papers, Box 107.

## Notes to Chapter 6

1. *Keighley News,* 11 October 1941.
2. Letter from Raymond Marriner to Kenneth Marriner, 10 April 1921.
3. *Kelly's Directory,* 1927.
4. *Wool Record,* 4 July 1957.
5. *The Yorkshire Textile Industry,* 1962.
6. *Wool Record,* 15 August 1957.
7. Lecture, News About Knitting, by James Norbury. Chief Designer, Paton & Baldwins, at the RSA 10 December 1959. Published by the International Wool Secretariat.
8. Companies House. Company No.: 00196149. Dissolved 19/12/1995.
9. *Keighley News,* 1 November 1985.
10. *Telegraph & Argus,* 30 October 1985.
11. Companies House. Company No.: 01693482. Dissolved 12 Dec. 1989.
12. D. T. Jenkins and K. G. Ponting, *The British Wool Textile Industry, 1770–1850,* 1987, p. 178.

## Notes to Chapter 7

1. *Keighley News*, 12 December 1955.
2. *Keighley News*, 12 December 1955.
3. Marriner Papers, Box 56.
4. *Keighley News*, 12 December 1955.
   notes to chapter 8
1. J. Lock and Canon W. T. Dixon, *A Man of Sorrow. The Life and Times of the Rev. Patrick Bronte. 1771–1861.* (1979).

# Sources and further reading

Anon., 1893, *The Century's Progress*.

Aspin, C., 1964, *James Hargreaves and the Spinning Jenny*.

Aspin, C., 1981, *The Cotton Industry*.

Baines, E., 2nd edition, 1966, *History of the Cotton Manufacture in Great Britain*.

Baines, E., 1970 (Reprinted with a new introduction by K. G. Ponting), *Account of the Woollen Manufacture of England*.

Baines, E., 1822, *History, Directory and Gazeteer of the County of York*, vols 1 and 2.

Baines, E., 1825, *History, Directory and Gazeteer of the County of Lancaster*.

Barfoot, P. and Wilkes, J., 1793, *The Universal British Directory*.

Briggs, A., 1952, 'Industry and Politics in Early Nineteenth Century Keighley', *The Journal of the Bradford Historical and Antiquarian Society*. Vol. VII. New Series.

Brown, G. H., 1896, *On Foot Round Settle*.

Cudworth, W., 1886, *Rambles round Horton*.

Daniels, G. W., 1920, *The Early English Cotton Industry*.

Dewhirst, I., 1974, *A History of Keighley*.

Dewhirst, I., 1975, *Yorkshire Through The Years*

Dodd, E. E., 1966/7, 'The Bradford Strike of 1825', *Bradford Textile Society Journal*.

Dumbell, S., 1923, 'Early Liverpool Cotton Imports and the Organisation of the Cotton Market in the Eighteenth Century', *Eonomic Journal*, vol. xxxiii, pp. 362–373.

Edwards, M. M., 1967, *The Growth of the British Cotton Trade*.

Fitton, R. I. and Wadsworth, A. P., 1958, *The Strutts and the Arkwrights, 1758–1830*.

Giles, C. and Goodall, I. H., 1992, *Yorkshire Textile Mills*.

Hallam, H. A. N., 1969, 'The Listers of Frizinghall', *The Bradford Antiquary. New Series, Part XLIV*.

Hatcher, J., 1985, *The Industrial Architecture of Yorkshire*.

Herbert, T. (ed.), 2000, *The British Brass Band – A Musical and Social History*.

Hodgson, J., 1879, *Textile Manufacture and other Industries in Keighley* (Facsimile reprint with introduction and index by Gillian Cookson and George Ingle 1999).

Ingle, G., 1974, *A History of R. V. Marriner Ltd, Worsted Spinners, Keighley*. M.Phil. thesis, Leeds.

Ingle, G., 1997, *Yorkshire Cotton*.

James, J., 1857, *History of the Worsted Manufacture in England*.

Jenkins, D. T., 1975, *The West Riding Wool Textile Industry, 1770–1835*.

Jenkins, D. T. and Ponting, K. G., 1987, *The British Wool Textile Industry, 1770–1850*.

Keighley, W., 1879, *Keighley, Past and Present*.

Lock, J. and Canon Dixon, W. T., 1979, *A Man of Sorrow. The Life and Times of the Rev. Patrick Bronte. 1771–1861*.

Miller, G. A., 1951, *Blackburn. The Evolution of a Cotton Town*.

Sheeran, G., 1993, *Brass Castles*.

Sigsworth, E. M., 1958, *Black Dyke Mills*.

Sigsworth, E. M., Spring, 1952, 'The West Riding Wool Textile Industry', *Wool Knowledge*, p. 16

Sigsworth, E. M., 1951/2, 'William Greenwood and Robert Heaton', *Bradford Textile Society Journal*, pp. 61–72.

Sigsworth, E. M., 1957/8, 'The End of Hand Loom Weaving', *Bradford Textile Society Journal*.

Smith, A., 2000, *Music Making in the West Riding of Yorkshire*.

Unwin, G., 1924, *Samuel Oldknow and the Arkwrights*.

Wells, F. A., 1972, *The British Hosiery and Knitwear Industry*.


*Bradford & Huddersfield Courier*

*Halifax Journal*

*Keighley News*

*Leeds Intelligencer*

*Leeds Mercury*

*Telegraph & Argus*

Bradford Reference Library

Cliffe Castle Museum, Keighley

*Commercial Directory for 1814–15* (Manchester)

Companies House

Keighley Reference Library

Marriner Papers, Business Archives, Brotherton Library, University of Leeds

Red House Museum, Kirklees Community History Service

West Yorkshire Archaeology Service (WYAS) Wakefield

*Wool Record.* 4/7/1957

*Woollen, Worsted and Cotton Journal.* Vol. 1.1853

Yorkshire Textile Archive, Bradford College

*Yorkshire Textile Industry*, 1962

# Index

References in **bold** are to illustrations. Readers should be aware that certain families carried through male first names from father to son